Shards of Glass:

A Comparison of Conservative and Liberal Minds

1

By: Dwayne D. Willis, MA, MSW

Table of Contents

Introduction:

For years I was a conservative, actually one could have called me a reactionary. I myself viewed my political views as more of a William F. Buckley conservative. One who argued from a position of logic rather than allow such a trifle thing as emotions figure into my debates. I could debate since Middle School; However, it was one teacher in High School who polished up my rough edges and mentored me into a skilled debater. This ability had the effect of driving my opponents absolutely insane. Here I was, their ideological enemy, yet I was polite and friendly in my arguments. In fact, I gained more friends that way. When someone asked me my secret, I would smile and say, "Never raise your voice, improve your argument."

But today, we have an entirely different atmosphere. Ideologically, we are split so many different ways. By race, country of origin, political view points, and even where we live determines our views and how we view the world. And today, I have slid all the way across the political spectrum to the left, far left. I now call myself a Democratic Socialist, mainly because of my 22 years spent in the trenches as a social worker, but even before that I spent five years in the Steelworkers union when I worked at the local steel mill. Over the years, I became increasing aware of the various economic disparities in our society, as well as our economic system. Good paying jobs in manufacturing was replaced by those in the service industry, which paid minimum wage or slightly above minimum. This recent economic downturn, which was due to the COVID-19 pandemic, literally decimated our economy. During the 2nd quarter of 2020, the Gross Domestic Product contracted by 32.9%. It should be noted here that anything more than a 10% contraction is considered a Depression.

The result is a considerable amount of economic anxiety. So much so, that the people of the United States started looking for a political party that best reflected their views and they thought could help them alleviate their fears. The Democrats were not used to the 10 second soundbite to convey their message, seeing that most of the problems the country faced couldn't be described in 10 seconds or less. But the Republican party seemed to master this. However, their message was the same. Cut the deficit, protect the second amendment, protect the fetuses, kick the lazy people off welfare, and the Blacks and Hispanics are coming to your neighborhood. As well as there's a lot of illegal immigrants pouring across the southern border, to take your jobs, kill your friends and family, as well as bringing tons of drugs into our country. If they are not stopped and stopped soon, America will not be the America you grew up in when you were young. It will become something totally unrecognizable.

Chapter One:

Imagine, if you will, a large arena filled to capacity with people. These people are being whipped into a frenzy by music. And finally, the speaker shows up, and the crowd goes wild! The speaker was saying everything that the crowd wants to hear, that foreigners are coming into the country and taking their jobs. The economy is in the tank, nobody respects us as a country anymore, the trade agreements are not advantageous to our country. Yet he is the only person who can fix the country and make it great again. Am I speaking of Donald Trump? Not at all. For I am speaking of Germany towards the end of the Weimar Republic and the raise of one Adolf Hitler.

No, this is not going to be a book about the rise of Hitler and everything he did, but rather an analysis of the people who voted for and instilled a fascist form of government which touched off a Second

World War, the murder of 6 million innocent Jews, and the deaths of countless men, women and children directly attributed to combat. Now, I know what you're thinking; At least he is not going to be writing about the United States. Right? Oh, you could not be further from correct.

Because you see, ever since the late 1960's and early 1970's, this country has been on a steady decline towards a state of fascism. One could argue the point that it started just after World War II, when thanks to Atomic Bomb, we became the world's first Superpower, complete with all the trappings and trimmings of an Empire. During the 1950's, when our biggest enemy was Soviet Russia, we always had in the back of our collective minds the possibility of Nuclear War, but in the meantime, the planet became a giant chessboard for the United States and the Soviet Union to attempt to prop up governments friendly towards us or take out governments which were not so friendly.

And all the while, the World War II veterans would wave their flags proudly and teach us youngsters (me being one of them,) of how precious freedom was. Those lessons were not lost on me. So almost 50 years later, I am starting to see similarities between history then and history now. But history does not exist in a vacuum, it takes people. Today's society is broken down by left- and right-wing politics, Black Lives Matter vs. Blue Lives Matter (or All Lives Matter,) Pro-Choice vs. Pro-Life, and Pro 2nd Amendment vs. Pro-Gun Regulation. These are just a few of our differences. This book is going to examine those differences, not so much on the Left end of the political spectrum, but we will address some, but we will focus more of our attention on the Right end of the political spectrum. It will be a sociological and psychological analysis of why the right wing is so willing to allow an authoritarian state come to power in this country and basically turn the once Beacon of Democracy into a Third World Banana

Republic. So, I bet you are wondering, is this going to be another trip down the rabbit hole? Of course, it is. But we are going to go deeper than we last journeyed down the rabbit hole when we analyzed the Culture Wars. Yes, you will be surprised with what I found just as much as I was surprised.

The right wing in this country is primarily concerned with four things in this country as they see it. Guns, as in the unrestricted ownership of all firearms, Gays, as in same sex marriage is an abomination to my fourth marriage, Abortion, as in we must make sure the all the precious little fetuses have a chance to be born, but after you're born, tough shit! I ain't gonna pay for any programs that might give you a leg up to allow you equal footing with my kids. Besides, if your mother wasn't such a whore, we wouldn't have this problem, (yes, I have actually heard someone say that to a child.)   And, last, but not least, God, as in we wouldn't have all these problems if they hadn't kicked God and prayer out of schools. Don't you think each one of these will be addressed during the course of my tome, and be prepared, people would much rather believe a convenient myth than an inconvenient truth. We are also going to talk about other races and prejudice head on. We are going to discuss the "family values," that conservative politicians love to incite crowds with are not the family values of today, but of years gone past, which is never going to return. We are going to talk about how conservative voters vote against their own self interests in respect to labor when it is wrapped up so nicely in issues, they deem important. Do I think I am going to change any conservative's minds? No, and I'll be explaining that as well. But think of this as an instruction manual on how to handle your obnoxious uncle at Thanksgiving, or the local Karens in your neighborhood. You know the ones, they are anti-vaccination because it contains a tiny amount of mercury, but will literally die if they cannot get to go to Appleby's for lunch during a pandemic while their waitress wears dons a mask for her own protection. And we are going to talk about the ever-widening gap between the haves and the have-nots. And anything else I choose to point out, because this is my book and I'll point out whatever I damn well please. And on that note, let's begin.

Chapter Two:

So why do Conservatives act and react like their world is falling to pieces all around them? Why is it that the elderly has become the most susceptible to all the fear mongering? Remember, these are the earlier Baby Boomers who were the hippies, the Yuppie couples of the 1980's, etc. These people supposedly had the power to change our nation, which they did, but not for the better. Well, it has something to do with evolution. You see, we all have a "lizard brain," which is our brain stem, which houses our most primitive mental functions, one of those is that of fear response. The more fear we are exposed to, the more our lizard brains respond.

The tendency of Republicans both to respond to and sow fear and panic has been with us for decades. Yet during the coronavirus pandemic, to anyone who bothers to look, we are seeing a new and strangely unremarked twist to their behavior, a development that gives valuable, and chilling, insight into Republican psychology.

Over the years, conservatives (I use the term interchangeably with Republicans) have swooned over various moral panics, such as the evergreen fear that gays will convert their children into perverts, or the imagined war against Christmas that secular humanists supposedly wage with the implacable ferocity of the Stalingrad campaign. Since 9/11, panic over Muslims has been a hardy perennial: the GOP faithful are forever on guard lest their city council should impose Sharia law on hapless Christians. Never mind that for the last decade, domestic right-wing terrorist incidents have greatly outpaced incidents committed by Muslims.

Republicans boast of Senator Tom Cotton of Arkansas as one of their up-and-coming brightest lights. A graduate of Harvard, he has nonetheless paid the price to become a bona fide future Republican candidate for president by making himself over as a Trump He passes with flying colors the requirement that future Republican aspirants for the presidency strut their stuff on Fox News, proving that they can lie with a straight face as convincingly as any Fox host. On that network recently, as Americans were suddenly confronting a life-and-death threat from coronavirus, Senator Cotton charged that "China has unleashed this plague on the entire world through their dishonesty and their lack of transparency and corruption." Even admitting there was no evidence for his claim, and ignoring at the moment that scientists had overwhelmingly dismissed it, Cotton burnished the rumor circulating among conservatives that China produced the virus as a bioweapon to be used against its adversaries. Senator Cotton's paranoia is but another example of the reptilian complex that characterizes today's Republican party, formerly the GOP – America's Grand Old Party.

During the early 1950s, Republicans stampeded themselves and much of the country into a state of hysteria over homegrown Communist subversion. That there were a few Communist spies is undeniable, but Republicans vastly overestimated their number. Senator Joseph McCarthy, the ringleader of the GOP vigilantes, was unable to uncover a single one, settling for ruining the reputations of innocent Americans.

Over the years, conservatives (Republicans, whatever,) have swooned over various moral panics, such as the evergreen fear that gays will convert their children into perverts, or the imagined war against Christmas that secular humanists supposedly wage with the implacable ferocity of the Stalingrad campaign. Since 9/11, panic over Muslims has been a hardy perennial: the GOP faithful are forever on guard lest their city council should impose Sharia law on hapless Christians. Never mind that for the last decade, domestic right-wing terrorist incidents have greatly outpaced incidents committed by Muslims.

There is a reason for these inappropriately fearful responses that is related to brain physiology. Strongly conservative individuals literally have different brains than the rest of the population. MRI tests have shown that different centers of the brain light up more robustly in these persons than others, and their amygdala – the so-called "lizard brain" that controls the threat response – is larger than average. To what extent this characteristic is an inherited tendency and to what extent socialization alters the highly adaptable components of the brain is debatable.

This is not to say that there are not powerful evolutionary reasons for a fight-or-flight response: some threats in our pre-history (say, an approaching saber-toothed tiger) were real. So is the instinct not to walk casually amid automobile traffic. But when fear is exaggerated and the response irrational it can impede long-term survival, for the human species needs to confront and intelligently overcome risk in order to progress above the level of feces-throwing primates.

Some aversion instincts are deeply wired in everyone, regardless of ideology: such as the impulse to avoid the sources of suspected infectious disease. This is so heavily ingrained that the mere sight of some disgusting object, such as a rotting animal corpse, will trigger the immune system to produce more antibodies. This even can occur from looking at pictures of sick persons.

All the more surprising, then, is the nonchalant response of most Republicans to the coronavirus pandemic. You'd think it would stimulate their lizard brains to hyper-alertness, but no.

From the president, who once said the virus was a hoax (then predictably denied that he said what he said) to Rush Limbaugh, who claimed it was only a common cold, to Congressman Matt Gaetz (a man who habitually acts like the insufferable smartass all of us encountered in the eighth-grade), who showed up on the House floor wearing a gas mask to mock the Democrats' concern, Republicans have demonstrated derision and indifference. Even the fact that many of them were exposed to, or even contracted, the virus at the annual CPAC convention has not improved their lackadaisical attitude. (That CPAC has transitioned from virally broadcasting noxious ideas to more literal virus spreading is an irony that future historians may note with bemusement.)

This behavior is not confined to GOP politicians and rabble-rousers. It began with anecdotal evidence that some Fox News-addicted elderly were not regarding the threat of the virus seriously and weren't taking personal protective measures. But polls have also found that there is a statistically significant difference between the reaction of ordinary Democrats and Republicans to the outbreak. A whopping 72 percent of Republicans trust the "information" provided by Trump, whose performance has been so abysmal, and so full of lies, that a child of eight could see through them.

It has been more than three and a half years now, and the shock has yet to wear off of the horror of President Trump, not for liberals not for moderates, and not even for some conservatives. In fact, once the Senate of the United States found him not guilty during his impeachment trial, Trump has become even more emboldened, acting like some third world dictator. Weekly, daily, sometimes hourly, Trump says or does things either on television or on social media which causes even his staunchest supporters at Fox News to cringe. Trump does something that liberals experience as not merely wrong or politically abhorrent, but something that violates all the norms and principles of public life that we hold most dear. He drives liberals crazy in ways that even Presidents Nixon, Reagan, and Bush never did. One of my favorite lines I have heard from his supporters is that "he speaks what's on his mind." If you translate that into English, it basically means "he hates the same people I do." Never since Richard Nixon, has an American President sowed such division among the American people, especially towards members of minority communities.

Why? What is it about Trump's personality, his followers, and the brand of authoritarian conservatism they share? And what is it about liberals that renders them so apoplectic in this situation? Pop psychologists and pundits have brushed up against these questions, but no one has quite wrestled them to the ground. We think we know why Trump makes liberals go berserk. The answer is only partly about Trump. It also has to do with the essential characteristics of liberal ideology and psychology, that is, the very qualities that make liberals "liberal." We'll get there, but first we need to establish a few points about conservatism, authoritarianism, Trump's personality, and the psychology of the liberal mindset.

Let us acknowledge that there is something human and intrinsically valuable about the "conservative" impulse to preserve social, economic, and political legacies. As the late Marxist philosopher Gerald A. Cohen pointed out, nearly all of us possess a "natural" bias in favor of existing value and are often heard bemoaning the fact that "things ain't what they used to be." When political conservatives tout the importance of the nuclear family or the Constitution or even American exceptionalism, they strike a chord that resonates with most if not all of us. Sure, I would like for things to be as they were when I was a child, a teen, or when I was coming of age in the 1980's. Things were simpler back then again, we had less responsibilities back then as well, and we seemed to have plenty of time to achieve my hopes and dreams. Now that we are closer to retirement than we were to our college days, and that some of us are grandparents, we long for a time long since passed that we could share, if only for a moment, with our grandchildren.

The understandable, even admirable reverence for tradition can, however, easily slip into more dangerous forms of ideological calcification that wittingly or unwittingly prop up existing forms of exploitation and oppression and stifle opportunities for progress, equality, and social change. Thus, Cohen added that he could never be a conservative about matters of social justice, "because what conservatives like me want to conserve is that which has intrinsic value, and injustice lacks intrinsic value (and has, indeed, intrinsic disvalue)." The challenge, for all of us living in a liberal democracy, is to distinguish clearly between elements of the societal status quo that possess intrinsic value and those that do not, and to conserve only the former. No doubt, this is more easily said than done. For instance, systemic racism has intrinsic disvalue, as it neither promotes the very causes it was supposedly meant to prop up, that is the social and economic classes of the Antebellum South, nor promotes a healthy discourse within our society.

What accounts for this astonishing behavior? I have written before about American conservatives' authoritarianism, a trait that has starkly accelerated during Trump's period of riotous misrule. This cultish instinct to blindly follow the direction of their leaders, and to conform their opinions to those of their own in-group, has become so strong that even in the face of disease it appears to have overridden even deep-rooted human aversion instincts, as well as their own habitual, hypertrophied sense of social fear.

The transcendent power of authoritarianism over immature minds can explain otherwise baffling incidents in history. Why did members of the Charlemagne assault battalion, Frenchmen who had no rational stake in Nazism or Germany, die by suicide in the rubble of Berlin, perishing to defend a Führer who considered France the hereditary enemy of Germany? Why do Republicans seem to think they have to scoff at a global pandemic in order to "own the libs?"

The GOP has not yet gone quite as far as the Charlemagne unit, but make no mistake: the core tenets of American conservatism in the age of Trump are genuinely crazy. If Republicans, goaded and cheered on by dangerous imbeciles like Rush Limbaugh or Sean Hannity, continue to maintain their grip of governmental power, the results will not be pretty.

One of the major takeaways I want to stress is that a conservative's lizard brain is larger than the general populations. That is why you see morbidly obese men parade around in cammos and semi-automatic weapons, because "Omar and Abdullah might decide to attack us here at the local Burger King." Some among us are very suspicious and rather paranoid of people who have skin color darker than a paper sack, sadly. When a black man or woman is murdered by the police, they are the first ones to say, "If you're not doing anything illegal, then the police won't bother you." What they forget is their interactions with police is far different than that of a Black or Hispanic person. What a lot of white people forget is that sometimes being Black or being Hispanic is enough of a crime to get someone killed.

More than any other political system,
democracy, as Plato pointed out long ago,
has the inherent ability to actualize its own
demise. By manipulating the democratic
process, elites can limit the freedoms of
individuals or social groups and put in place
leaders who are not democratically inclined.
In a very concrete sense, democracy
depends upon ordinary citizens' capacities
and motivations to absorb democratic values
and tolerate those with diverse social,
cultural, ethnic, and ideological
backgrounds. These are precisely the values
that those on the right wing have been
attacking for years, and they have exploited
the inherent popularity of conservative
ideology to do so. In other words, if we do
not continually fight for equality for all, then
one day, we all could see that none of us are
equal, in any way.

Chapter Three

So, what about conservatism and religion?
As I said in one of my previous works,
America is the only nation on Earth where
politics, religion, and economics have been
mixed together in an "unholy trinity."
Where if you are conservative and rich, God
must have shown his divine providence
upon you for being such a fine, moral
person. This is a throwback to the
Calvinistic interpretation of religion, and its
modern-day equivalent, Prosperity gospel.
Conservative evangelicals were
understandably concerned in 2013 when the
IRS held up tax-exempt applications for
certain groups, asking questions specifically
related to prayer meetings. The question was
not about the content of prayers, however
but the purpose. Arguments about the
separation of church and state aside, the fact
that something is said in a religious setting
doesn't mean it isn't political speech.

"Pulpit Freedom Sunday," an annual event by conservatives protesting an IRS ban on political endorsement by churches that are tax-exempt, for example, "transubstantiates" partisan politics into religious worship "so that the two elements became a new act."

Jesus' command to "render to Caesar the things that are Caesar's, and to God the things that are God's" sounds straightforward, but religion, especially the Religious Right have long since abandoned their pursuit of what is God's and are now focused on obtaining what is Caesar's. Ever since the 1980 Presidential election where Jerry Falwell's Moral Majority basically installed Ronald Reagan as President in hopes of getting Roe v. Wade overturned did religious conservatives scored a major victory at the ballot box. With every Presidential since, religious conservatives have "waved the bloody shirt (it's a Post-Civil War term, Google it if you want to know more,) in order to get a Republican elected to the White House. But what really sent religious conservatives over the edge was the (false) rumor the President Barack Obama was a Muslim. Now, they failed to read the United States Constitution, where it said that "no religious test shall be administered to hold public office." And if that wasn't enough, they also accused him of not being born in a foreign country (like Kenya.) Again, they failed to read the Constitution, namely the 14th Amendment, which grants "birthright" citizenship. Seeing that his mother was a US citizen, who never renounced her citizenship, President Obama could have been born on Mars and would still be considered a US native born citizen. It is a sad commentary of this country where we fear anything new, different, or out of the ordinary. We used to achieve things, great things, before we got so scared, so afraid to venture forth. Those same people who used to have the world in their hands, now cower in fear over anything, and I do mean anything, that could upset their world, or at least their view of it,

Princeton political scientist Fred I. Greenstein has cautioned about the uses of personality in analyzing political activity; in fact, he directly addressed "the tangled history of studies of authoritarianism." He noted, however, that while the study of authoritarian personalities once seemed to be at a "dead end," that has proven not to be the case. Rather, "in the 1980s an ingenious and rigorous program of inquiry by Altemeyer (1981, 1988) furnished persuasive empirical evidence that the original authoritarian construct was an approximation of an important political-psychological regularity--the existence in some individuals of an inner makeup that disposes them to defer to authority figures."

These, of course, are followers. Altemeyer labeled these people "right-wing authoritarians" not because he was looking to target political conservatives, but rather because he was drawing broadly on the historical terms that identify those who openly submit to established authorities, and whether those authorities are political, economic or religious, those who submit to them are traditionally described as being on the right wing. As Altemeyer developed and refined his testing, however, it became apparent that those who tested as highly submissive to economic or religious authorities also proved to be hard-right political conservatives.

In addition to being especially submissive to established authority, Altemeyer's research revealed that those he calls right-wing authoritarians also show "general aggressiveness" towards others, when such behavior is "perceived to be sanctioned" by established authorities. Finally, these people are always highly compliant with the social conventions endorsed by society and established authorities. These basic traits, submissiveness to authority and conventionality, are the essence of those Altemeyer describes as right-wing authoritarians. If these traits are not present in some significant (albeit varying) degree, he does not consider the subject to be a right-wing authoritarian. However, these people can, and often do, consistently reveal they have many other interesting traits as well.

Based on Altemeyer's study, as well as those of other social psychologists, I prepared a list of the additional traits that these personalities, both men and women who test high as right-wing authoritarians, often evidence: highly religious, moderate to little education, trust untrustworthy authorities, prejudiced (particularly against homosexuals, women, and followers of religions other than their own), mean-spirited, narrow-minded, intolerant, bullying, zealous, dogmatic, uncritical toward their chosen authority, hypocritical, inconsistent and contradictory, prone to panic easily, highly self-righteous, moralistic, strict disciplinarian, severely punitive, demands loyalty and returns it, little self-awareness, usually politically and economically conservative/Republican.

So now we are starting to see a particular sociological and psychological profile coming together which displayed some of the traits of a right-wing authoritarian or someone who is inclined to follow said authoritarian.

Much of the work on authoritarianism focused on followers, and only in recent decades have social psychologists developed tests to measure the traits of authoritarian leaders, or as Altemeyer states, "person who wanted to be submitted to." These people, because of their inclination and desire to dominate others and to dominate social situations in which they find themselves, are said to have a "social dominance orientation," given their take-charge natures.

The term "social dominance orientation" may sound like academic jargon, but actually it is highly descriptive of the personalities of many who run social and political situations and organizations--the leaders who insist on running the show. The word "social," of course, refers to the general organization of society; "dominance" relates to control or command over other people; and "orientation," as used here, means their inclination or disposition. These are people who seize every opportunity to lead, who enjoy having power over others, and who will seek it both fairly and not so fairly.

People who test high as social dominators are also economically conservative and have little tolerance for equality. They consistently agree when asked about statements such as the following: "Some people are just more worthy than others"; "This country would be better off if we cared less about how equal all people were";

and "To get ahead in life, it is sometimes necessary to step on others." In addition, they will respond in the negative to the proposition that "All humans should be treated equally."

Again, I have prepared a listing of the traits revealed in the testing of these remarkably manipulative and cunning personalities, who are typically men: dominating, opposes equality, desirous of personal power, amoral, intimidating and bullying, faintly hedonistic, vengeful, pitiless, exploitive, manipulative, dishonest, cheats to win, highly prejudiced (racist, sexist, homophobic), mean-spirited, militant, nationalistic, tells others what they want to hear, takes advantage of "suckers," specializes in creating false images to sell self, may or may not be religious, usually politically and economically conservative/Republican. Does any of this sound like a certain President we all know.

These lists of traits for both right-wing authoritarian followers, and social dominating authoritarian leaders, should be understood as not necessarily describing every person who falls into the type. While many have all the traits, not all will have all, or even most, of them. Most people who test high as authoritarians, whether followers or leaders, have some of these traits, however.

Professor Meyer-Emerick wants to know if there are genetic tendencies that promote what she dubs "authoritarianism." She defines this distasteful quality through the work of University of Manitoba associate professor of psychology Robert Altemeyer. He's developed a helpful questionnaire, the Right-Wing Authoritarian (RWA) Scale, to identify those harboring authoritarian tendencies.

According to Professor Altemeyer, right-wing authoritarians are cognitively rigid, aggressive, and intolerant. They are characterized by steadfast conformity to group norms, submission to higher status individuals, and aggression toward out-groups and unconventional group members. On the RWA Scale, subjects are asked to agree or disagree with statements like: "Some of the worst people in our country nowadays are those who do not respect our flag, our leaders and the normal way things are supposed to be done" and "There is absolutely nothing wrong with nudist camps." Guess which one RWAs tend to agree with?

Meyer-Emerick notes that high RWAs perceive the world as a significantly more dangerous place than those who score low. High RWAs are more submissive to government authority and indifferent to human rights. They also tend to be more hostile and more highly punitive toward criminals, and more racially and ethnically prejudiced, and religious, to boot. In the United States, guess what? Republicans cluster at the high end of the RWA Scale whereas Democrats range across the scale.

Researchers at the University of California at Berkeley essentially confirmed this view with a meta-analysis of scores of academic studies on conservative political attitudes last year. In the study, "Political Conservatism as Motivated Social Cognition," the Berkeley researchers found common psychological factors linked to political conservatism include: fear and aggression, dogmatism and intolerance of ambiguity, uncertainty avoidance, need for cognitive closure, and terror management that causes conservatives to shun and even punish outsiders and those who threaten the status of their cherished world views. The researchers did half-heartedly assure readers that their findings do not mean that "conservatism is pathological or that conservative beliefs are necessarily false, irrational, or unprincipled." Which I totally disagree with my learned colleagues on this one fact. If one examines the recent domestic terrorist attacks, church shootings and the like, the entire, 100% of the attacks have been carried out, not by Muslims, not by Hispanics, not by Blacks, but by right wing extremists.

Altemeyer, inventor of the RWA Scale, believes that there is no such thing as a Left-Wing Authoritarian. "I do not think 'an authoritarian impressively like the authoritarian on the right' reposes on the left end of the RWA scale. Rather the contrary," Altemeyer declared. In fact, Altemeyer finds that low RWAs are "fair-minded, even-handed, tolerant, nonaggressive persons…They score low on my prejudice scale. They are not self-righteous; they do not feel superior to persons with opposing opinions."

Studies using other authoritarianism instruments that are not obviously confounded with political orientation have produced similar results. Some studies have employed a simple child rearing measure about the importance of obedience (e.g. 'Obedience and respect for authority are the most important virtues children should learn'). Although this measure has some methodological shortcomings, it has been included in the American National Election Studies, because it is thought to be devoid of political content, Azevedo et al. found that scores on the child rearing measure predicted social, economic, and overall conservatism in a large sample of American respondents (with rs ranging from .16 to .27).

Even more convincingly, Sprong et al. conducted a cross-national investigation of the desire for strong leadership in 28 countries from North and South America, Western and Eastern Europe, South and North Asia, the Middle East, and Oceania. Items used to measure this construct (e.g. 'Our country needs a strong leader right now') contained no specific ideological referents. Nevertheless, the desire for strong leadership was indeed correlated with right- (versus left-) wing self-placement at $r = .20$, and this correlation was robust in a multilevel model ($p < .001$) that adjusted for numerous individual-level and country-level characteristics (e.g. respondent sex, subjective and objective indicators of inequality, democracy scores, and homicide rates).

Another panelist, Charles Anthony Smith, a lawyer and Ph.D. candidate in political science at the University of California at San Diego, explored evolutionary biology explanations for how these unsavory RWAs arose in our midst. In his talk, "Law, Leadership, and Lords: Machiavellian Intelligence and the Role of Obedience in Collective Action," Smith suggested that the propensity to obey would be adaptive in either attacking or defending groups. Those groups which could more quickly be organized to defend themselves would be more likely to survive. A deliberative outlook under such circumstances would be an evolutionary disadvantage. Smith believes that this evolutionary tendency toward obedience can explain a host of behaviors, including the initial rise of theocracies in which leaders manipulated the propensity to obey by claiming that the gods had given them the divine right to rule.

Smith believes this tendency also explains the "rallying around" effect that occurs during attacks and wartime. Smith noted that polls taken on September 7-10, 2001, gave President Bush only a 51 percent approval rating, whereas his approval rating had jumped to 81 percent on September 15. The same phenomenon occurred after the Oklahoma City bombing under President Clinton and after the Marine barracks were blown up in Lebanon under President Reagan. He asked the not-unreasonable question, "Why do we rally around them when our leaders fail?" Smith evidently believes that evolution has hardwired humans to react that way.

In contrast to Smith's suggestion that certain tendencies might be hardwired into human beings, Altemeyer believes that children learn right-wing tendencies through harsh discipline from their parents. However, studies looking at identical twins reared apart back up the notion that political attitudes are heritable. They find that on average, about 60 percent of the individual differences that we observe in scores on a version of the Wilson-Patterson Conservatism Scale (WPC) are attributable to genetic individual differences. The WPC is a catch phrase test in which subjects are asked to indicate whether they approve of various topics, such as the death penalty, X-rated movies, women's liberation, foreign aid, abortion and so forth by circling YES or NO. Obviously, such tests have no ability to handle nuances, or grapple with the reasons someone might have for harboring attitudes that the researcher dubs "conservative," or even "authoritarian."

Whether it be an unfortunate evolutionary holdover or a mental disease transmitted by our parents—the science is apparently still up in the air—academic researchers have surely amassed enough evidence of psychopathology that conservatism can listed in the next edition of the Diagnostic and Statistical Manual of Mental Disorders (DSM-V TR?). Reasonable people, such as the distinguished academic researchers cited here, will no doubt agree that until effective treatments can be developed, we should reconsider whether sufferers of conservatism, like other mental defectives, should be allowed freely to exercise the franchise.

Ever since the publication of The Authoritarian Personality, a subset of scholars has energetically contested the notion that there is an authoritarian-conservative nexus. Some have argued, largely on the basis of historical events in the Soviet Union, Cuba, and other totalitarian socialist systems, that authoritarianism, as a psychological construct, is equally compatible with leftist and rightist ideological manifestations One problem with this view is that it fails to distinguish clearly between the characteristics of individual personalities and social systems.

Another issue concerns the presence of content overlap between measures of authoritarianism and political orientation. To the extent that there is such overlap, and in some cases, there surely is, correlations between authoritarianism and conservative (or right-wing) orientation could be artificially inflated. For example, Altemeyer's RWA scale contains items such as 'You have to admire those who challenged the law and the majority's view by protesting for women's abortion rights, for animal rights, or to abolish school prayer' (reverse-scored) and 'God's laws about abortion, pornography and marriage must be strictly followed before it is too late, and those who break them must be strongly punished'. These items conflate authoritarian attitudes with conservative positions on specific issues, such as women's rights, abortion, and marriage equality. This content overlap could produce a spurious correlation between authoritarianism and conservatism.

Recently, Conway, Houck, Gornick, and Repke proposed a new scale to measure 'left-wing authoritarianism' (LWA). By rewriting RWA items so that they would be more attractive to liberals and progressives in the U.S., these researchers repeated and even exacerbated methodological problems associated with earlier versions of the RWA scale. In particular, they deliberately confounded authoritarian inclinations and support for liberal (as opposed to conservative) opinions and groups in society. The LWA scale includes items such as: 'Progressive ways and liberal values show the best way of life'; 'It's always better to trust the judgment of the proper authorities in science with respect to issues like global warming and evolution than to listen to the noisy rabble-rousers in our society who are trying to create doubts in people's minds'; and 'There is absolutely nothing wrong with Christian fundamentalist camps designed to create a new generation of fundamentalists' (reverse-scored). Given that the items refer explicitly to liberal causes, such as environmentalism, and conservative causes, such as religious fundamentalism, it is hardly surprising that their endorsement is strongly correlated with political orientation in the expected manner

But there are other problems as well. In adapting items from the RWA scale Conway et al. added more barrels to existing items, many of which were already multi-barreled.

At the same time, they presented no
evidence concerning the factor structure or
validity of the LWA scale. When Hoffarth et
al. administered the LWA scale to new
convenience samples of Americans, they
discovered that LWA scores were negatively
correlated with intolerance of ambiguity and
the endorsement of authoritarian attitudes
about child rearing. Conway et al.'s
instrument may tap into liberal concerns
(and attitudes about epistemological and
moral relativism), but there is no evidence
that it measures authoritarianism per se.

Other research programs have instead
focused on developing (and validating) more
psychometrically sound and ideologically
neutral measures of authoritarianism. For
instance, Duckitt et al. reworked
Altemeyer's items to remove content
overlap between authoritarianism, on one
hand, and conservatism and religiosity, on
the other (e.g. 'Our leaders should be
obeyed without question' and 'What our

country really needs is a tough, harsh dose of law and order'). Dunwoody and Funke likewise created new items that were devoid of conservative and religious language (e.g. 'We should believe what our leaders tell us' and 'Strong force is necessary against threatening groups'). Studies employing these scales confirm the existence of an authoritarian-conservatism nexus in the U.S., Australia, and the U.K.

So, in a nutshell, the left and the right are completely different on their views on authoritarianism. The right uses it in an attempt to establish order and conformity within society. While the left does it in order to reallocate limited resources for the greater good, as well as promoting some semblance of equality and social justice. Am I saying that all right winger is evil and all left wingers are saints? No, not at all. But in today's political climate, which side is parading around state capitol grounds with

semi-automatic weapons in an attempt to
intimidate people?

Chapter Four:

Weak minds discuss people; average minds discuss events; strong minds discuss ideas," said Greek philosopher Socrates. People and events dominate public discourse because they matter to the bread and butter issues of the people. But then, as Jesus Christ said, man does not live by bread alone. He needs ideas, "God's word," according to Jesus. We need strong minds to germinate transformative ideas.

And those ideas are sorely lacking. No longer is critical thinking and intellectual discourse part of the American Public-School curriculum, but rather subjects are taught now so students will be able to practice mental regurgitation at the end of the school year upon standardized tests year after year until graduation, in order to keep the state Department of Education from taking over the school district.

I read recently that a young man required a
permission slip to read Ray Bradbury's
Fahrenheit 451, in high school. I do not
recall the young man's age, but what stood
out to me was the fact that his father was a
writer on one of those satirical comedy/news
shows on television, and the irony of book
censorship about a novel about book
censorship was not lost on him. I too, had to
sign permission slips for my children to read
either Brave New World or 1984, I do not
recall which. But all three of these books I
read in high school and reread them for the
pure pleasure of it, and just because it said
an occasional "shit" or "damn," and there
were some adult situations (like sex,) in
them, but nothing I would classify as worthy
of censorship. Now, when I wrote my first
book, All our Hands are Stained, I sprinkled
the f—bomb so liberally throughout the
book, it was like parsley on a baked potato.
But these youngsters, and some older folks,
need to sit down and read these works about
a dystopian future. Because if we do not

tend to our country's future, our Republic is
doomed.

There will be times when humanity yearns
for such ideas. The coronavirus pandemic is
one such occasion when the world is
desperately looking for fresh ideas to shape
its future. Unfortunately, I fear that there are
a great many people who would much rather
die than have to switch to a "new" normal.
They would happily long for the old days,
pre-pandemic, when they could go where
they wanted, eat where they wanted, go
drinking where they wanted, all without a
mask and fear of contracting something that
could kill them.

Historically, Europe has been the intellectual
kernel of mankind. Several avant-garde
ideas originated in the minds of European
philosophers and thinkers. In the last few
centuries, all the important political ideas
that impacted the world extensively came
from Europe. From John Locke's
Enlightenment thinking to Karl Marx's

Marxism, from the Utilitarianism of Jeremy Bentham and John Stuart Mill to the Social Contract tradition of Thomas Hobbs, from Edmund Burke's Conservatism to Frederick Nietzsche's Nihilism, Europe produced many grand political ideas in the last two centuries. The democratic institutions that evolved during the same period are also the product of the continuous churning in Europe's intellectual milieu.

One grand idea that India contributed to world political thought in the last century was Mahatma Gandhi's non-violence. From Martin Luther King Jr to Nelson Mandela to Barack Obama, the list of leaders who admired and adopted non-violence as a political ideology is long. Interestingly, after India's successful experimentation with non-violence in 1947, dozens of countries adopted it and subsequently secured independence. Most of those countries became democracies and the world witnessed a "democracy boom" by the end of the last century. The collapse of the erstwhile Soviet Union and the end of the Cold War also helped further democratization.

But the dawn of the 21st century saw matters drifting fast. Democratic deficit and fatigue are setting in with alarming speed. Authoritarian regimes have bounced back with a vengeance. Terrorism, that acquired new dimensions and legitimacy towards the end of the last century, has led to the resurgence of the politics of violence. The first quarter of the 21st century witnessed the rise of "wolf warriors" and "lone wolfs".

It is in this political climate that the Covid-19 has struck the world. It has affected all existing political systems, authoritarians and democrats alike, diminishing the credibility of each one. A leaderless and rudderless world is emerging out of these two-decades of churning culminating in the pandemic. What the post-pandemic world needs is not just a new leadership, but also ideas for a new world order.

Regarded for long as the crown jewel of democratic liberalism, the United States (US) is yielding ground quickly and significantly, signaling the decisive decline of those values in the world. In the last three decades, at least two dozen countries have turned authoritarian. But somehow the word, liberalism became connected to the word Socialism and is used interchangeably by the right wing. Any idea which may or could improve everyone here in the United States is viewed as socialism, anything that might benefit minorities in this country is viewed as socialism. Today's right wing is dedicated to one thing; Preservation of life as they remember it from the 1950's, the Baby Boomer's Glory Years. All aspects of it, including racial segregation. They fear Blacks and Hispanic males, and females to some extent. They fear their culture, music, words, everything. They only want to live in a world that looks, sounds and behaves like they do. They want their children and grandchildren to grow up in a similar world. And they are willing to vote into office and incompetent strongman in order to achieve their vision of security.

Authoritarian regimes such as China have emerged powerful during the same period. Authoritarianism does not affect the people of the respective countries alone. It puts a lot of pressure on others too. Democracies, by very nature, become vulnerable to the onslaught of authoritarianism. In the process, they too gradually turn to authoritarian measures to ward off the challenge of authoritarian regimes. The net result will be a world less liberal and less democratic.

There is a silver lining in the cloud though. Authoritarian regimes, although seemingly dominant at the moment, cannot sustain themselves for long. China is ageing fast. The one-child norm of the 1980s and 90s has skewed its demography. In a decade's time, it will turn into an evening economy. So will other authoritarian regimes in West Asia for a variety of reasons. With their financial fortunes plummeting due to falling oil revenues, these authoritarian sponsors of terrorism are wilting precariously.

The next 10 years will be crucial for the world. It has to not only build new leadership, but also come up with new ideas and agendas.

It is here that India has a golden opportunity. India's handling of the Covid-19 crisis has revealed the brighter side of its leadership and society. The combined efforts of the government led by Prime Minister Narendra Modi, extensive efforts by its ubiquitous bureaucracy, and the exemplary discipline and commitment of its 1.3 billion people have helped India manage the pandemic in a manner that has set an example to others.

So, depending upon the outcome of the 2020 Presidential campaign as well as when the pandemic ends, and trust me, every pandemic in human history has ended and after every pandemic the human race has to recalibrate going forward. The Black Death in Europe caused a severe labor shortage, which the old feudal system could no longer address, so guilds, the forerunners of the modern labor union, came into being. So, this is what we will have to deal with going forward.

Chapter Five:

One ambitious attempt to understand the
''culture war'' from a psychological

perspective is the theory of moral
foundations. This work is predicated on the
metatheoretical assumption that previous
research in moral psychology has focused
too narrowly on allegedly ''liberal'' values
of ''justice, rights, and welfare.'' What is
needed, according to moral foundations
theorists, is to move ''beyond Kohlberg's
ethic of justice and Gilligan's ethic of care,''
classic approaches to moral psychology that
Haidt has dismissed as products of ''liberal
bias.'' Moral foundations theorists argue for
an ''alternative approach to defining
morality that does not exclude conservative
and non-Western concerns,'' one that
incorporates values and orientations that
have nothing to do with justice, rights, or
welfare.

Accordingly, moral foundations theorists identify ''five groups of virtues'' that are said to explain why liberals and conservatives often hold divergent opinions on moral issues. Consistent with their framework, studies involving college student and internet samples reveal that liberals are significantly more likely than conservatives to prioritize principles of fairness and the avoidance of harm, whereas conservatives are more likely than liberals to regard ingroup loyalty, deference to authority, and purity (or sanctity) as morally significant. A crucial, albeit untested assumption of moral foundations theory is that ingroup, authority, and purity concerns—which are referred to as ''binding foundations'' are ''moral (instead of amoral, or immoral).'' This assumption is part of a broader agenda to incorporate more conservative ideas in social psychological research under the rubric of increasing ''political diversity.'' Moral foundations theorists sometimes suggest that they are offering a purely descriptive theory about what people believe is moral (rather than what actually is moral), but their frequent use of terms such as ''virtues,'' ''moral truths,'' ''moral worth,'' and ''moral knowledge'' clearly implies normative, prescriptive conclusions.

Moral foundations theorists commonly chastise liberals for failing to understand or appreciate conservative moral motivations; there is even said to be a '''moral color-blindness' of the left'' has also advanced a ''moral taste bud'' metaphor in which liberals are likened to hapless chefs who believe falsely that they can serve meals based on only one or two ''taste buds''—as opposed to ''all five.'' These are clearly normative (and not merely descriptive) arguments, whether their proponents realize it or not.

Research on moral foundations pushes ethicists to ''move beyond an individualist-consequentialist framework and take conservative ideas seriously.'' And in explaining the political significance of research on moral foundations, Haidt writes that, ''morality is not just about how we treat each other (as most liberals think); it is also about binding groups together, supporting essential institutions, and living in a sanctified and noble way.'' Many of these claims are critical, evaluative, and prescriptive in nature,

But contrary to popular assumptions, this does not mean that they are necessarily impervious to empirical confrontation. It is possible that the endorsement of ''conservative'' (as opposed to ''liberal'') moral values is indeed more conducive to live a virtuous (or noble) life, whether or not moral foundations theorists actually subscribe to such a hypothesis.

Of course, it is also possible that the opposite is closer to the truth. The existing evidence marshaled in support of moral foundations theory does not adequately address the issue, because it focuses on purely subjective considerations (what liberals and conservatives believe to be morally relevant), without any attempt to scrutinize the validity of those subjective considerations. We cannot ignore innate human instincts and cultural conditioning, but anyone who wants to think seriously about morality must be prepared to evaluate such motives from an independent point of view that is achieved by transcending them. This article takes one, admittedly small and ultimately unsatisfying. step in this general direction of distinguishing between subjective conceptions of morality (which are, after all, indistinguishable from mere moralizing) and morality from a more independent, objective perspective.

To illustrate the claim that conservatives are motivated by moral concerns that liberals do not sufficiently understand, appreciate, or respect, (former) Republican Senator Rick Santorum, whose ''anti-gay marriage views were based on concerns for traditional family structures, Biblical authority, and moral disgust for homosexual acts (which he had previously likened to incest and bestiality).'' Conservative opposition to gay marriage, in other words, should be understood in terms of principled moral commitments to defending the norms and traditions of the ingroup, respecting conventional authority figures, and enforcing standards of purity and divinity suggested that many of the allegedly ''moral'' characteristics ascribed to conservatives by moral foundations theorists possess a striking resemblance to authoritarianism, as conceptualized by political psychologists over the last 70 years.

Decades of research find that the "authoritarian personality,'' which is characterized by conventionalism, submission, and aggression, is associated with ethnocentrism (or ingroup favoritism), sexism, homophobia, and punishment of social deviants. This work provides scientific grounds for doubting the claims made by moral foundations theorists that deference to authorities and traditional conventions should be considered ''moral (instead of amoral, or immoral).'' Such work also casts a more worrisome light on liberals should embrace more of the ''binding foundations'' in their political messaging campaigns. As 'actual moral system, no matter how heinous, seems capable of being modeled by some weighting of the moral intuitions.

To clarify our position, we are by no means suggesting that ''liberal'' attitudes or orientations are above moral reproach or that conservatism is synonymous with authoritarianism or that all conservative positions on moral issues are motivated by intergroup hostility. At the same time, there are several decades' worth of data demonstrating that, throughout the Western world. conservatism (or right-wing orientation) is robustly correlated with authoritarianism, prejudice, and discrimination against members of disadvantaged groups.

 Conservatism is also positively associated with social dominance orientation, which is conceptualized as a generalized preference for group-based hierarchy and the maintenance of inequality.

Social dominance orientation, in turn, predicts sexism, racism, classism, homophobia, and a wide range of prejudicial outcomes. Studies suggest that authoritarianism and social dominance orientation, when taken in conjunction, explain approximately half of the statistical variability in generalized prejudice.

Do Authoritarianism and Social Dominance Orientation Explain Liberal-Conservative differences in ''Moral'' Intuitions? Is it possible that liberal-conservative differences in moral intuitions are attributable to differences in authoritarianism and social dominance? There is reason to suspect that they are. In addition to the obvious parallels between heightened ingroup, authority, and purity concerns and the two types of ''authoritarian personalities,'' It was found that ingroup, authority, and purity themes were significantly more common in the narratives of individuals who scored high (vs. low) on right-wing authoritarianism and, to a weaker extent, social dominance authoritarianism was positively correlated with endorsement of the ''binding foundations'' but did not adequately address the implications of these correlations for their descriptive or prescriptive conclusions about morality and politics.

There is indeed a reasonably close empirical connection between authoritarianism and social dominance orientation, on one hand, and the subjective consideration of ingroup loyalty, obedience to authority, and purity as moral virtues, on the other hand.

Authoritarianism, social dominance, and conservative moral intuitions share key psychological antecedents, such as perceptions of a dangerous world—consistent (rather than inconsistent) analysis of political conservatism as motivated social cognition. Second, two large surveys of undergraduate students and reported that scores on a right-wing authoritarianism scale were strongly and positively correlated with endorsement of ingroup, authority, and purity concerns,

whereas scores on a social dominance orientation scale were negatively correlated with concerns about fairness and avoidance of harm. Third, another study analyzed results from a large, nationally representative sample of citizens in New Zealand and observed that (a) right-wing authoritarianism and social dominance orientation was positively correlated with the endorsement of ingroup, authority, and purity concerns, and (b) social dominance orientation was negatively correlated with the endorsement of fairness and avoidance of harm.

Despite the relatively close and consistent empirical connections between ''conservative'' moral intuitions and the two types of ''authoritarian personality,'' previous authors, for the most part, have refrained from challenging the pivotal assumption that ingroup, authority, and purity concerns are ''moral (rather than immoral or amoral).'' None of the earlier articles included quantitative analyses bearing on the question of whether liberal-conservative differences in moral intuitions are attributable to (or statistically mediated by) individual differences in authoritarianism and social dominance. We investigated this mediational hypothesis in a study that combined samples of student and internet respondents. In one of the samples, we were able to explore the hypothesis, which has also been neglected in previous research, that endorsement of ''binding foundations'' would be associated with hostility and support for discrimination against outgroups such as Muslims, foreigners, and immigrants—outcomes that most ethicists would be hard-pressed to describe as moral (rather than amoral or immoral).

So why the concern with social dominance? Well, if you are a student of history, which for any of you who have purchased my previous books, know that I am a huge history Geek, white males have predominately dominated the American culture since the first settlement before we were a nation. It was they who brought slaves into this country. I know, you're going to protest and say that there were white slaves in this country as well. To that I resoundingly reply, "Bullshit!" The reason for my response is because of this is twofold; 1.) The white "slaves" were in fact, indentured servants who agreed to work for a certain period of time in exchange for his/her passage to this country, even when the contract was up, they received a small stiped to get started. 2.) During this time period, Irish, Italians, and other southern Europeans were not even considered less than human, and were given jobs no one else wanted, (sound familiar?) but they were paid just a fraction of what, "Good English" were paid. So no, there were no such thing as "white slaves," in this country. So, I wish conservatives would stop using that excuse as a justification for slavery.

Chapter Six:

Now that in the first five chapters of this book we talked about the sociological aspects of Conservatives and their gravitating towards authoritarianism, I would like to spend the rest of the book (don't worry, there's only ten chapters,) discussing the psychological aspects of a Conservative and attempt to answer why they have a tendency to gravitate towards an authoritarian regime.

I suppose we could always look at Germany in between the First and Second World Wars. With is I am going to paint with as wide a brush as possible. Germans are phenomenal engineers and architects. They love stability and order. Under the Kaisers and with the early years of Hitler, the German people had a very stable, orderly society. Just the way they like it. However, during the years after the Treaty of

Versailles, which demanded a complete
demilitarization and for Germany to pay
high reparations to the Allied powers. This
threw the German economy into a state of
hyper-inflation, where it took a wheelbarrow
of German Marks just to buy a loaf of bread.
During this period was also Germany's
foray into Democracy, in the form of the
Weimar Republic. It was a mere shell of
Germany's former military and industrial
glory. The German people were broken and
defeated, and their economy was in ruins.
These events sowed the seeds for Hitler and
his National Socialist Party, to start making
end roads into the Berlin Government until
1933 when the party won enough seats in
the Reichstag and Hitler was named
Chancellor of Germany with the promise of
"making Germany great again." Of course,
we all knew how that turned out.

My point is that Hitler, like Trump, played
upon the fears of the people over
immigrants, gypsies, homosexuals, and last

but certainly not least, the Jews as the source of Germany's problems. Donald Trump during the 2016 Presidential campaign, he blamed China for taking American Jobs and he promised he would bring American jobs back. He pointed the finger at immigrants coming across the border bringing drugs and crime into this country. He would say the "only he could solve" the problems in this country. And that he would "Make America Great Again," a phrase which he had copyrighted in 2012 after the election of Barack Obama to a second term as President.

However, once he became President, the shit show began. He had worked diligently to reverse or overturn every action President Obama did, up to and including the Affordable Care Act. But one lone Senator, the late John McCain of Arizona, who was suffering from terminal brain cancer, put country over party and cast a "no" vote, effectively torpedoing any hope of overturning the ACA. As a result, Trump resorted to his favorite method of temper tantrum, Twitter, to attempt to bluff and bully his way of being correct. He followed the advice of one of his advisors, one Stephen Miller, who is well known in white supremacist, for his policy on handling illegal immigration. One of the key components was the policy of family separation, where the children of those immigrants and incarcerated in cages, with no medical care, no bathrooms, no bedding, and very little human contact. Animals in an animal shelter are treated better than these innocent children. The reasoning behind this policy? To act as a deterrent to keep families, even refugees from attempting to enter the country.

Stephen Miller is one of those individuals whose life was tainted by reactionary philosophy. When he was college, he started associating with several white supremacists who convinced him that the Black, Hispanic and Muslim peoples were all responsible for America's ills, and they either should be ran out of the country or killed outright in order to make America what it was meant to be; a haven for the white race.

Am I the only one who sees the mental illness going on here? I see narcissism, and anti-social personalities in both men. The problem is, one cannot treat a personality disorder, one can only minimize its impact. But now there is hope for the followers of Trump, lest we fall into the trap which Germany fell into, and suffer the possible end result if we do not get this addressed.

t has practically achieved the state of an axiom in our field that liberals are more complex

thinkers than conservatives. This is not without reason. Meta-analyses, covering a vast array of evidence related to dogmatism, uncertainty avoidance, openness to experience, need for closure, and integrative complexity, suggest that liberals are indeed more complex than conservatives

Nonetheless, we believe that the judgment that conservatives are broadly simple-minded may be premature.

Participants were randomly assigned one of three versions of the dogmatism scale. Some participants received the standard version of the scale as typically used in previous research on ideology.

Other participants received one of two domain-specific versions of the scale. In one condition, participants received a scale that was designed to measure their dogmatism about religion, and in another condition, participants received a scale designed to measure their dogmatism about environmental issues.

These domain-specific dogmatism scales were nearly identical to the standard scale and to each other, but they differed only in intentionally injecting content domains into the items (please see the online supplemental information for the entire scales). An example will help illustrate. A standard item on the dogmatism scale is "A group which tolerates too much difference of opinion among its own members cannot exist for long." For the religious dogmatism scale, this item was adapted (italics and bold added for emphasis here) to say "A religious group which tolerates too much difference of opinion among its own members cannot exist for long." The parallel environmental dogmatism questionnaire item read "An environmental group which tolerates too much difference of opinion among its own members cannot exist for long."

In this way, the two-alternate domain-specific dogmatism questionnaires kept almost all of the

language from the original items but interjected a content domain (either religion or environmental issues) into the majority of those items.

These results suggest that the relationship between ideology and dogmatism is domain-specific.

Conservatives are indeed more dogmatic on the religious domain; but liberals are more dogmatic on the environmental domain.

It might be easy to dismiss these effects as reflecting the content preferences of liberals and conservatives (and thus as not reflecting anything about dogmatism per se). There are two reasons why we think such a dismissal would be premature.

First, the dismissal is a double-edged sword. If the question is "do prior results suggest that conservatives are more dogmatic?" then simply dismissing our results as only having to do with content raises the possibility that all dogmatism scales are picking up on content primarily (and not dogmatism per se).

Second, more importantly, a quick dismissal of these findings does not capture the subjective

nature of the items themselves. For example, consider that for dogmatism, liberals scored higher on the following questions:

There are two kinds of people in this world: those who are for the truth that the planet

is warming and those who are against that obvious truth. When it comes to stopping global warming, it is better to be a dead hero than a live coward.

A person who thinks primarily of his/her own happiness, and in so doing disregards the

health of the environment (for example, trees and other animals), is beneath contempt.

We did this because the current conceptual case being made is that conservatives are simple-minded. Because the slope of the line in a correlation might not fully capture differences between persons on each side of the liberal/conservative divide, there is value in considering what people who classify themselves as being on the "conservative" side of the ledger are like, as compared to those on the "liberal" side, in more categorical terms. Persons who scored above the midpoint were categorized as conservative, while those below the midpoint were categorized as liberal.

Now do I mean that conservatives are in some way less smart than liberals? Depends on what your definition of smart is? Some can tear down an engine and rebuild it, while others can program a computer, while others still can build a house without blueprints. So just because someone is gifted either right or left brained is not a sign of a lack of intelligence. In this case, I am going to show it is simply how the brain is hardwired.

Chapter Seven

What does make liberal's and conservative's brains so different? Here is a possible answer:

On January 27, 2011, from a stage in the middle of the San Antonio Convention Center, Jonathan Haidt addressed the participants of the annual meeting of the Society for Personality and Social Psychology. The topic was an ambitious one: a vision for social psychology in the year 2020. Haidt began by reviewing the field that he is best known for, moral psychology. Then he threw a curveball. He would, he told the gathering of about a thousand social-psychology professors, students, and post-docs, like some audience participation. By a show of hands, how would those present describe their political orientation? First came the liberals: a "sea of hands," comprising about eighty per cent of the room, Haidt later recalled. Next, the centrists or moderates. Twenty hands. Next, the libertarians. Twelve hands. And last, the conservatives. Three hands.

Social psychology, Haidt went on, had an obvious problem: a lack of political diversity that was every bit as dangerous as a lack of, say, racial or religious or gender diversity. It discouraged conservative students from joining the field, and it discouraged conservative members from pursuing certain lines of argument. It also introduced bias into research questions, methodology, and, ultimately, publications. The topics that social psychologists chose to study and how they chose to study them, he argued, suffered from homogeneity. The effect was limited, Haidt was quick to point out, to areas that concerned political ideology and politicized notions, like race, gender, stereotyping, and power and inequality. "It's not like the whole field is undercut, but when it comes to research on controversial topics, the effect is most pronounced," he later told the researcher.

Haidt was far from the first to voice concern over the liberal slant in academia, broadly speaking, and in social psychology in particular. He was, however, the first to do it quite so visibly—and the reactions were vocal. At first, Haidt was pleased. "People responded very constructively," he said. "They listened carefully, took it seriously. That speaks very well for the field. I've never felt as if raising this issue has made me into a pariah or damaged me in any way." For the most part, his colleagues have continued to support his claims—or, at least, the need to investigate them further. Some, however, reacted with indignation.

The critique started with data. True, there was little doubt that conservatives in the world of psychology are few. A 2012 survey of social psychologists throughout the country found a fourteen-to-one ratio of Democrats to Republicans. But where were the hard numbers that pointed to bias, be it in the selection of professionals or the publication process, skeptics asked? Anecdotal evidence, the Harvard psychologist Daniel Gilbert pointed out, proved nothing. Maybe it was the case that liberals simply wanted to become professors more often than conservatives. "Liberals may be more interested in new ideas, more willing to work for peanuts, or just more intelligent," he wrote. The N.Y.U. political psychologist John Jost made the point even more strongly, calling Haidt's remarks "armchair demography." Jost wrote, "Haidt fails to grapple meaningfully with the question of why nearly all of the best minds in science find liberal ideas to be closer to the mark with respect to evolution, human nature, mental health, close relationships, intergroup relations, ethics, social justice, conflict resolution, environmental sustainability, and so on."

The views on the other side are equally strong. When I asked Paul Bloom, a psychologist at Yale who edits the journal where Haidt's paper will appear, what he thought of the research, he pointed out what he believed to be a major inconsistency in the field's responses. "There's often a lot of irony in this area," he said. "The same people who are exquisitely sensitive to discrimination in other areas are often violently antagonistic when it comes to political ideology, bringing up clichéd arguments that they wouldn't accept in other domains: 'They aren't smart enough.' 'They don't want to be in the field.'"

The Nobel Prize-winning behavioral economist Daniel Kahneman called Haidt's work "great" and "a real service." The University of British Columbia psychologist Steven Heine pointed out, "Science benefits from diverse perspectives, and key advances often occur when ideas slip across disciplinary borders. But many invisible norms and practices in a field can discourage the mingling of diverse ideas." Political homogeneity, he went on, comes at "a substantial cost" to research quality. Conservative viewpoints, the Florida State University psychologist Roy Baumeister added, "would inform and elevate how we understand a huge part of life and of culture."

By its own admission, the field of social psychology has a very liberal slant, warding off the more conservative thinkers. So, what does this do in terms of research and teaching philosophy? Well, it taints it and skews it towards a liberal interpretation of the data collected on a given project. Have I done this, no, but I have read studies where one could tell that the interpretation of the results of the data collected was interpreted in an unusual fashion? Remember, I practiced for 22 years in the field of social work, and read a considerable amount of research studies, since social work is considered to be the applied social science, and we apply research from the other social sciences to be able to do our jobs.

In the mid-2000s, a political scientist approached the neuroscientist Read Montague with a radical proposal. He and his colleagues had evidence, he said, that political orientation might be partly inherited, and might be revealed by our physiological reactivity to threats. To test their theory, they wanted Montague, who heads the Human Neuroimaging Laboratory at Virginia Tech, to scan the brains of subjects as they looked at a variety of images, including ones displaying potential contaminants such as mutilated animals, filthy toilets, and faces covered with sores. to see whether neural responses showed any correlation with political ideology. Was he interested?

Montague initially laughed at the idea, for one thing, MRI research requires considerable time and resources, but the team returned with studies to argue their case, and eventually he signed on. When the data began rolling in, any skepticism about the project quickly dissolved. The subjects, 83 in total, were first shown a randomized mixture of neutral and emotionally evocative pictures, this second category contained both positive and negative images, while undergoing brain scans. Then they filled out a questionnaire seeking their views on hot-button political and social issues, in order to classify their general outlook on a spectrum from extremely liberal to extremely conservative. As Montague mapped the neuroimaging data against ideology, he recalls, "my jaw dropped." The brains of liberals and conservatives reacted in wildly different ways to repulsive pictures: Both groups reacted, but different brain networks were stimulated. Just by looking at the subjects' neural responses, in fact, Montague could predict with more than 95 percent accuracy whether they were liberal or conservative.

The subjects in the trial were also shown violent imagery (men pointing revolvers directly at the camera, battle scenes, car wrecks) and pleasant pictures (smiling babies, beautiful sunsets, cute bunnies). But it was only the reaction to repulsive things that correlated with ideology. "I was completely flabbergasted by the predictability of the results," Montague says.

His collaborators, John Hibbing and Kevin Smith at the University of Nebraska at Lincoln, and John Alford at Rice University, in Houston, were just as surprised, though less by the broad conclusion than by the specificity of the findings and the startling degree of predictability. Their own earlier research had already yielded a suggestive finding, indicating that conservatives tend to have more pronounced bodily responses than liberals when shown stomach-churning imagery. However, the investigators had expected that brain reactions to violent imagery would also be predictive of ideology. Compared with liberals, they'd previously found, conservatives generally pay more attention, and react more strongly, to a broad array of threats. For example, they have a more pronounced startle response to loud noises, and they gaze longer at photos of people displaying angry expressions. And yet even in this research, Hibbing says, "we almost always get clearer results with stimuli that are disgusting than with those that suggest a threat from humans, animals, or violent events. We have an ongoing discussion in our lab about whether this is because disgust is simply a more powerful and more politically relevant emotion or because it is an emotion that is easier to evoke with still images in a lab setting."

Findings so dramatic, especially in the social sciences, should be viewed with caution until replicated. The axiom that extraordinary claims demand extraordinary proof clearly applies here. That said,

Hibbing, Montague, and their colleagues are scarcely alone in linking disgust and ideology.

At a deep, symbolic level, some researchers speculate, disgust may be bound up with ideas about "them" versus "us," about whom we instinctively trust and don't trust.

Using a far cruder tool for measuring sensitivity to disgust—basically a standardized questionnaire that asks subjects how they would feel about, say, touching a toilet seat in a public restroom or seeing maggots crawling on a piece of meat— numerous studies have found that high levels of sensitivity to disgust tend to go hand in hand with a "conservative ethos." That ethos is defined by characteristics such as traditionalism, religiosity, support for authority and hierarchy, sexual conservatism, and distrust of outsiders. According to a 2013 meta-analysis of 24 studies, pretty much all the scientific literature on the topic at that time—the association between a conservative ethos and sensitivity to disgust is modest: Disgust sensitivity explains 4 to 13 percent of the variation in a population's ideology. That may sound unimpressive, but it is in fact noteworthy, says David Pizarro, a psychology professor at Cornell who specializes in disgust. "These are robust, reliable findings. No matter where we look, we see this relationship"—a rarity in the fuzzy field of psychology. The trend stands out even more, he adds, when you consider all the other things that potentially impinge on "why you might have a particular political view."

Broadly speaking, studies of possible connections between ideology and susceptibility to disgust fall into two categories. The first involves measuring subjects' sensitivity to disgust as well as their social or political ideologies and then calculating the correlation between the two. The second category explores whether exposure to disgusting subject matter can actually influence people's views in the moment. But whatever the type of study, the same general finding keeps turning up. "We are at the point where there is very solid evidence for the association," says Michael Bang Petersen, a political scientist at Aarhus University, in Denmark. His own research finds that "disgust influences our political views as much as or even more than long-recognized factors such as education and income bracket."

So many scientists have thrown themselves into this line of research in recent years that it has become an accepted discipline, sometimes jokingly given the aptly unappetizing name "Disgustology." Their conclusions raise a lot of questions, chief among them: Why in the world would your reaction to mutilated animals, vomit, and other unwelcome things somehow be associated with your views on transgender rights, immigration, or anything else stirring debate in the news?

Researchers have theories rather than answers. At a deep, symbolic level, some speculate, disgust may be bound up with ideas about "them" versus "us," about whom we instinctively trust and don't trust. In short, this research may help illuminate one factor—among many—that underlies why those on the left and the right can so vehemently disagree.

There is nothing inherently political about disgust. It evolved not to guide us at the ballot box but rather, it is widely theorized, to protect us from infection. As we move about in the world, a sizable volume of research shows, our minds are constantly searching our surroundings for contaminants—moldy leftovers, garbage spilling out of trash cans, a leaky sewage pipe—and when the brain detects them, it triggers sudden feelings of revulsion. Confronted, we withdraw from the threat.

The mechanism is part of what's known as the "behavioral immune system," and it is as vital for survival as the fight-or-flight response. Our pathogen-tracking system does its job largely beneath our conscious awareness—and pays close attention to those walking germ bags we call human beings.

This dynamic was highlighted in a pioneering series of experiments launched in the early 2000s by the psychologist Mark Schaller, of the University of British Columbia. Like a smoke detector, Schaller discovered, our germ radar operates on a better-safe-than-sorry principle. It is error-prone in flagging danger—it produces a lot of false positives. Any physical oddity displayed by the people around us—contagious or not—can set off an alarm. Just as a pink eye, a hacking cough, or an open wound may activate our behavioral immune system, so too can a birthmark, obesity, deformity, disability, or even liver spots.

Furthermore, having germs on our mind can affect how we feel about people we perceive to be of a different race or ethnicity from ourselves.

In one notable experiment, Schaller showed subjects pictures of people coughing, cartoonish-looking germs sprouting from sponges, and other images designed to raise disease concerns. A control group was shown pictures highlighting threats unrelated to germs—for instance, an automobile accident. Both groups were then given a questionnaire that asked them to assess the level of resources the Canadian government should provide to entice people from various parts of the world to settle in Canada. Compared with the control group, the subjects who had seen pictures related to germs wanted to allocate a greater share of a hypothetical government advertising budget to attract people from Poland and Taiwan— familiar immigrant groups in Vancouver, where the study was conducted—rather than people from less familiar countries, such as Nigeria, Mongolia, and Brazil. Familiarity does make a difference. Schaller, whose landmark studies are credited with sparking the initial interest in the relationship between disgust sensitivity and prejudice, says: "If I grow up in an environment where everybody looks pretty much the same, then someone from China, for example, might trigger my behavioral immune system. But if I grow up in New York City, then a person who comes from China is not going to trigger this response."

If pathogen cues of this kind can indeed intensify prejudice, the explanation could be biological adaptation. Some scientists—notably the psychologist Corey Fincher, at the University of Warwick, in England, and the biologist Randy Thornhill, at the University of New Mexico—theorize that foreigners, at least in the past, would have been more likely to expose local populations to pathogens against which they had no acquired defenses. Other scientists think germ fears piggyback on negative stereotypes about foreigners common throughout history—the notion that they're dirty, eat bizarre foods, and have looser sexual mores.

Whatever the explanation, an online study launched by Petersen and Lene Aarøe, also at Aarhus University, and Kevin Arceneaux of Temple University suggests that a dread of contagion is not just a personal matter. It can have an impact on society. The investigators began by evaluating the disgust sensitivity of nationally representative samples of 2,000 Danes and 1,300 Americans. The participants were then asked to fill out a questionnaire that assessed their views about foreigners settling in their respective countries. As the researchers reported in 2017, opposition to immigration in both the Danish and American samples increased in direct proportion to a participant's sensitivity to disgust—an association that held up even after taking into account education level, socioeconomic status, religious background, and numerous other factors.

The team expanded the part of the study that focused on the U.S. It got state-by-state breakdowns of the prevalence of infections, and also analyzed statistics compiled by Google Trends, which tracks internet searches related to contagious illnesses in an effort to spot early signs of outbreaks. Crunching the numbers (the results are as yet unpublished), the researchers found that resistance to immigration is greatest in states with the highest incidence of infectious disease and where worry about this, as reflected by internet activity, has also been high.

More recent investigations by Petersen and Aarøe suggest that those with high disgust sensitivity tend to be leery of any stranger, not just foreigners. They view casual social acquaintances with a certain amount of suspicion—a robust finding replicated across three studies with a total of 4,400 participants. The implication is clear: Disgust and distrust are somehow linked. And maybe, again, the link is defensive in origin: If you shrink your social circle, you'll reduce your exposure to potential carriers of disease.

interest in disgust sensitivity extends beyond its potential role in fostering xenophobia and prejudice. As the social psychologists Simone Schnall, at the University of Cambridge, and Jonathan Haidt, at NYU, have shown, disgust sensitivity may also help shape beliefs about right and wrong, good and evil. In one experiment, Schnall, Haidt, and other collaborators sat subjects at either a clean desk or one with sticky stains on it as they filled out a form that asked them to judge the offensiveness of various acts, such as lying on a résumé, not returning a wallet found on the street, and resorting to cannibalism in the aftermath of a plane crash. One subgroup of participants seated at the filthy desk—those with high "private body consciousness," meaning they were particularly sensitive to their own visceral reactions—judged the transgressions more severely than those seated at the pristine desk.

Foul odors can be just as effective as a sticky desk. Another experiment involved two groups of subjects with similar political ideologies. One group was exposed to a vomitlike scent as the subjects filled out an inventory of their social values; the other group filled out the inventory in an odorless setting. Those in the first group expressed more opposition to gay rights, pornography, and premarital sex than those in the second group. The putrid scent even inspired "significantly more agreement with biblical truth." Variations on these studies using fart spray, foul tastes, and other creative disgust elicitors reveal a consistent pattern: When we experience disgust, we tend to make harsher moral judgments.

In thinking about why disgust sensitivity may be associated with conservative moral values, researchers have considered the potential connection between the behavioral immune system and religion. Religious strictures and other traditions may have the hidden function of protecting us from disease, some theorize. Our urge to respect certain culinary practices, sexual prohibitions, and injunctions about washing and hygiene may not be just about achieving spiritual or symbolic purity, but may be the result of an evolutionary drive to avoid contamination.

Could a predilection toward revulsion indicate how we vote? A team led by Cornell's David Pizarro and Yoel Inbar, at the University of Toronto, set out to answer that question by conducting an online study during the 2008 U.S. presidential contest between Barack Obama and John McCain.

In the run-up to the election, the researchers assessed the contagion anxiety of 25,000 "demographically and geographically diverse" Americans and then surveyed the attitudes toward the candidates held by a random subset of the larger group. Those with the highest germ fear reported that they were more likely to vote for McCain, the Republican nominee and the more conservative candidate. Further, the actual proportion of votes that went to him in each state directly scaled with that state's level of contagion anxiety. The researchers eventually extended studies of this kind to 121 countries and found that disgust sensitivity correlated with a conservative ethos basically everywhere there were sufficient data for analysis. As Pizarro, Inbar, and the other authors of the study write in the journal Social Psychological and Personality Science, this result suggests that disgust sensitivity "is related to conservatism across a wide variety of cultures, geographic regions and political systems."

Disgustology (their word, not mine,) is a young endeavor. Not all the pieces fit together neatly, and some suppositions (as always) may turn out to be wrong. But a few clues have recently surfaced that suggest a useful framework for interpreting this sprawling mass of findings. One of them, in hindsight, is obvious: the etymology of disgust. The English word is derived from the Middle French desgoust, which literally means "distaste." As it turns out, what tastes foul to us is typically a sour or bitter substance—which can be a marker of contaminants (think of spoiled milk). Several years ago, Pizarro learned that people vary tremendously in the number of bitter receptors they possess on their tongue, and thus in their taste sensitivity. What's more, the trait is genetically determined. This got him wondering: If conservatives have a greater disgust sensitivity, are they also better at detecting bitter compounds? "It seemed like a really long shot," Pizarro says. But he, Inbar, and Benjamin Ruisch, a grad student at Cornell, decided to put the idea to the test. They recruited 1,601 subjects from shopping malls and from the Cornell campus and gave them paper strips containing a chemical called Prop and another chemical called PTC, both of which taste bitter to some people. Sure enough, those who had self-identified as being conservative were more sensitive to both compounds; many described them as unpleasant or downright repugnant. Liberals, on the other hand, tended not to be bothered as much by the chemicals or didn't notice them at all.

The researchers went a step further. Taste receptors, they knew, are concentrated in fungiform papillae—those spongy little bumps on your tongue. The greater the density of papillae, the more acute your taste. So, they dyed subjects' tongues blue (which allows the papillae to be more easily observed), pasted a paper ring on them like those used to prevent pages from tearing out of a metal binder (to create a standard area to be evaluated), and recorded the number of circumscribed papillae. The degree to which subjects' views tilted to the right was, they found, in direct proportion to the density of papillae on their tongue. This result may have bearing on a puzzling partisan split in food preferences. A 2009 survey of 64,000 Americans revealed that liberals chose bitter-tasting arugula as their favorite salad green more than twice as often as conservatives did. It may also have a bearing on conservative President George H. W. Bush's famous hatred of broccoli—an unusually bitter vegetable. Of course, sometimes a stalk of broccoli is just a stalk of broccoli.

No doubt your own political allegiances will heavily influence what you extract from the bulk of this research. If you're liberal, you may be thinking, So. this explains some of the other side's nativism and hostility to immigration. But it's just as easy to flip the science on its head and conclude, as conservatives might, that the left is composed of clueless naïfs whose rosy-eyed optimism about human nature. and obliviousness to various dangers, will only lead to trouble.

The research itself does not speak to the relative merits of a conservative or liberal ethos, how could it? Conservatism and liberalism are not monolithic, and they rest on deep intellectual traditions. In terms of gut reactions, the relative appeal of each philosophy can depend significantly on context, for instance, on whether times are kind or cruel. When tensions are high and groups split into factions, as they inevitably do, we can depend on our family and friends to defend our interests, but the outsider is an unknown quantity and, from an evolutionary perspective, may be seen as a source of contamination or, more generally, a threat.

One defining characteristic of disgust, though, is that it occupies a blind spot in our psyche. As Pizarro notes, "It's such a low-level, almost noncognitive emotion that you really aren't thinking that much about it." Compared with anger, happiness, and sadness, he says, disgust is also "less open to change based on your judgment, your thoughts, your reasoning." Chocolate in the shape of dog poop, he points out, is still gross. The emotion is more reflexive than reflective. "That is the rhetorical strength of disgust," Pizarro says. "It's a little hack. You hack into brains pretty quickly and easily by making them feel disgust," bypassing logic and reason to sway judgment.

Aristotle may not have found this idea surprising. As he intuited millennia ago, a human being "is by nature a political animal," uniquely endowed with the capacity for deliberation and speech, but at the same time governed by instincts we share with other living creatures. Like bees, he noted, we have a desire to congregate, to form societies. Aristotle could not have anticipated the germ theory of disease, or the role infection avoidance might unconsciously play, but his fundamental insight about the animal side of our politics remains prescient. Even the most rational among us might not always be as rational as we'd like to think.

Chapter Eight

Republicans and Democrats differ in the neural mechanisms activated while performing a risk-taking task.

Republicans more strongly activate their right amygdala, associated with orienting attention to external cues. Democrats have higher activity in their left posterior insula, associated with perceptions of internal physiological states. This activation also borders the temporal-parietal junction, and therefore may reflect a difference in internal physiological drive as well as the perception of the internal state and drive of others.

"Punishment" refers to an event in which a subject chose a risky decision and lost. The results show that there were no significant differences in the behavior of Republicans and Democrats. Now, for those of us of a certain age and location (primarily in the South and Midwest,) punishment is acquainted with physical (or corporal) punishment, that was sometimes accompanied by mental or even emotional abuse. It is when the child reaches adulthood and starts having children of his/her own, they can choose one of two possible outcomes. They either perpetuate the cycle towards the next generation (normally the conservative path,) or they tend to take a more Laisez-faire approach to punishment and follow the "natural and logical consequences" model, (typically taken by most liberals.)

The insula and amygdala often function together in processing situations of risk and uncertainty. The amygdala plays a critical role in orienting of attention to external cues and fear conditioning; however, this structure is also important for other emotional information processing and behavior. Functional neuroimaging studies have shown amygdala activation in reward related processing, encoding of emotionally salient information, risk-taking, processing positively-valanced stimuli, and appetitive/aversive olfactory learning. In comparison, neuroimaging studies of insular cortex have observed critical involvement of this neural structure in pain, interoceptive, emotion-related, cognitive, and social processing. In particular, the insular cortex is important for representation of internal bodily cues crucial for subjective feeling states and interoceptive awareness. That differences in the processing of risk and uncertainty differentiate liberals and conservatives suggests an alternative way of conceptualizing ideology.

It is important to note the insula region observed in the current study is very posterior and borders the temporal-parietal junction. This region has been conceptualized as vital for "theory of mind" in processing, or the perception of others as thinking entities. In fact, a meta-analysis of over 200 fMRI studies on social cognition, the temporal-parietal junction was shown to be related to understanding immediate action intent in others. This suggests that the posterior insula activation found in the current study may reflect internal physiological drive as well as the perception of the internal state and drive of others.

A critical unresolved problem common to studies of the formation of ideology on both individual and institutional levels is the process through which a high dimensional space of distinct values, preferences, or issues is reduced to a low dimensional ideological space. It is even less clear why voters and their representatives in government should organize political attitudes into apparently constrained bundles that are relatively consistent over time. While it has been suggested that biological factors may lead liberals and conservatives to have different sets of politically relevant values, the evidence presented here suggests that the neural processes of evaluation themselves are distinct, perhaps reflecting differentiable values, as well as differing preferences for issues, candidates, and parties.

The strongest finding to come out of the "Michigan school" when the behavioral revolution spread to political science in the 1950s was that parents socialize their children to identify with the same political parties that they do. In fact, the correlation between parent and child is "so familiar and well established" that it is often taken as one of the few "axioms" of political science. Indeed, a simple model of partisanship that includes mother's and father's party accurately predicts about 69.5% of self-reported choices between the Democratic and Republican party. A classifier model based upon differences in brain structure distinguishes liberals from conservatives with 71.6% accuracy. Yet, a simple two-parameter model of partisanship using activations in the amygdala and the insular cortex during the risk task significantly out-performs the longstanding parental model, correctly predicting 82.9% of the observed choices of party.

One intriguing remaining puzzle regards the direction of causality. One might infer that the differing brain structures identified by Kanai et al. suggest genetic foundations for the differences in ideology. However, recent work has shown that changes in cognitive function can lead to changes in brain structure. For instance, applicants who worked to learn the map of London in order to pass a knowledge test required of potential cab drivers demonstrated significant growth in their hippocampus, a brain region related to memory formation.

Although genetic variation has been shown to contribute to variation in political ideology and strength of partisanship, the portion of the variance in political affiliation explained by activity in the amygdala and insula is significantly larger, suggesting that

acting as a partisan in a partisan
environment may alter the brain, above and
beyond the effect of the heredity. The
interplay of genetic and environmental
effects may also be driving the observed
correlations between the size of brain
regions and political affiliation. Further
untangling the roles of party, ideology,
genes, and neurocognition will be essential
for advancing our understanding of political
attitudes and behavior. The ability to
accurately predict party identification using
only neural activity during a risk-taking task
suggests that investigating basic
neuropsychological differences between
partisans may provide us with more
powerful insights than the previously-
available traditional tools of psychology,
sociology, and political science.

What Democrats and Republicans don't
have in common goes far beyond the ballot
box. Their personalities, like their core

beliefs and policy ideas, are fundamentally different.

Liberals are creative and curious, and tend to be more open to new experiences, while conservatives are more anxious, dislike change, and appreciate order in their lives. Scientists don't know if political interests shape temperament, or vice versa, but new research suggests lawmakers' personality traits play an important role in political causes, like forcing a government shutdown, and may even determine if those causes survive. It should be noted here that the Republican party has. In recent years, at least since the Reagan administration, as the party of fiscal responsibility, slashing programs (usually social safety net programs but never the Defense budget,) and cutting taxes (a move that only benefits corporations and a very few Americans.) They would always beat their campaign drums and tell the voters that the Democrats were nothing but a bunch of "tax and spend" liberals.

However, in recent years, starting in about 1993, with the election of Bill Clinton to the White House, did they start such foolishness, and Clinton was the last President to successfully balance the budget. However, even President since has done one thing consistently. If the Presidency was held by a Republican, the deficit was higher than the Empire State Building. Former Vice President Dick Cheney famously remarked, "Deficits don't matter," when putting the "War on Terror," on a credit card, deferring it from being added to both the deficit as well as the National debt. President Obama finally added the war costs into the deficits and the results were depressing! But, to President Obama's credit, he successfully cut the deficit in half before leaving office. Now his successor, Donald J. Trump has skyrocketed the National debt through both a massive tax cut (primarily for the wealthiest 1%,) as well as provided 4 Trillion dollars for economic relief for the COVID-19 pandemic and the resulting financial depression. As of the writing of this book, Congress is in negotiations over another relief package, that will total put somewhere between 1 and 3 Trillion dollars.

In a study published in the journal Psychological Science, researchers asked 300 people in an online survey whether they agreed or disagreed with both political ("In general, I support labor unions") and nonpolitical statements ("I enjoy coffee"). They also asked participants to indicate how much others who shared their political views would support their attitudes.

The results showed that liberals underestimated their levels of partisan support; that is, they thought their beliefs were different from their liberal peers, when they actually were not. Conservatives and moderates, on the other hand, thought their beliefs were more similar to those of other members of their political group than they actually were, overstating partisan agreement. These patterns of thinking held for topics unrelated to politics, like personal preference for coffee.

Author's Note: Not only do I enjoy coffee, I LOVE COFFEE! All kinds, all brands, I do not discriminate (especially with doughnuts!)

American liberals and conservatives use different parts of their brains when assessing risks, a new study finds.

A new study says that the brains of American Democrats and Republicans are wired differently, and that they use entirely different sections when making risky decisions.

Let the debates (and jokes) commence.

Liberals show a higher level of activity in the left insula, a portion of the brain associated with self-awareness, social cues, addiction, emotional processing, empathy, and even orgasms (insert Bill Clinton joke here).

Conservatives, on the other hand, tend to weigh risk in the right amygdala, an area of the brain that aids in survival, including reacting to violations of personal space and controlling social interaction, fear, and aggression (insert Dick Cheney joke here).

Different types of brain activity among Democrats and Republicans during risk-taking tasks underscores fundamental differences in the U.S. dual-party system.

Republican philosophy is grounded in the basic rights granted to individuals, and thus they tend to support smaller government, fewer regulations, and more personal empowerment. Because Republican thought is centered in the part of the brain that deals with the evolutionary fight-or-flight response, it makes sense that their platform centers on issues of national defense, such as securing our borders and beefing up the military.

Democrats, however, are often crusaders for the greater good, advocating for civil rights, fair play, and a national security strategy based on alliances. This jibes with the basic functions of the insula, where their risk assessment takes place. Whether or not specific members of these parties stick to these ideals is a different discussion altogether.

The standard in political science has been to use a person's environment, namely which side of the fence Mother and Father sat on, but researchers claim that's only accurate about 70 percent of the time. Monitoring brain activity, however, provides 83 percent accuracy, the researchers stated.

U.S. politics are serious business. In the 2012 election cycle, both parties spent more than $985 million each, according to an assessment by The New York Times.

With so much at stake, the science behind politics can be used to predict voter behavior, as well as to guide campaign strategy.

The ability to accurately predict party politics using only brain activity while gambling suggests that investigating basic neural differences between voters may provide us with more powerful insights than the traditional tools of political science.

Whether the right amygdala or the left insula is in play. Trump made quick use of the Republican's fears and fight or flight responses during the 2016 Presidential campaign. He painted a picture of roving bands of illegal immigrants killing, raping and pillaging the countryside. He stated that our military was a joke and that it had been cut to the point where the United States could no longer defend itself against another attack by the "Muslims," and that his predecessor left the United States in a financial mess. But he assured the crowds at these "Nuremberg" rallies, that he and only he could solve the nation's problems. He

was going to be a "Law and Order,"
President (to borrow a line from Richard M.
Nixon,) but when a true crisis hit, he failed
to listen to the Doctors and scientists who
knew far more about plagues and pandemics
than anyone else in the country. Trump
immediately went on the attack towards
China, calling the virus such things as, "The
Chinese Virus," The Wuhan Virus," and the
worst one of all in my opinion, "Kung Flu."
Of course, anyone with any intelligence had
a good chuckle and really started taking the
Coronavirus seriously. They started taking
steps to protect themselves and their loved
ones. But he stated that," He took no
responsibility at all," should things start
going wrong. And shortly thereafter, they
did. As the body count steadily rose and the
economy was basically had the brakes put
on it. Trump started saying the we need to
get the economy open again, as he thought
the stock market continuing to go up was the
only economic indicator he needed to worry
about. But not so fast, another economic

indicator, which was far more important to his election chances, was about to come calling. And I am speaking of the Unemployment rate. Suddenly, since we had a service-oriented economy with no one to provide services to, so businesses shut their doors, some permanently. And literally for 21 weeks, over one million people filed for first time unemployment claims. The Gross Domestic Product, which is the measure of all goods and services produced in the United States contracted 32.9% in the second quarter of 2020, the largest in history. Oh, and as a side note, a contraction of just 10% is considered an Economic Depression.

Well, all the governors of the states threw back open their economies and guess what happened? Yes, there was a resurgence in infections. This was true especially in those states with Republican governors, in particular, Texas, Georgia, Florida, and Arizona. Only California, which has a

Democratic governor has also experienced a spike in Coronavirus cases. Of course, the 4 Republican led states were trying to toe the party line, believing that the virus was a lot less dangerous than it really is. I supposed perceived threats, rather than real one, are the only ones Republicans recognize.

Now, Americans have been conditioned to fear Blacks, Muslims, Hispanics, Chinese and Japanese peoples. But not so much the Chinese and Japanese peoples. Muslims (as well as Indians and Sikhs, are included in this as well,) due to their dark skin, accents, and their dress. This was true especially after 9/11/2001, when attacks upon these groups escalated, but quickly subsided. Except for Muslims, who continue to be viewed with mistrust and some scorn. If you examine some newspapers and TV news reports, you might find planning commissions denying land use permits to Muslim groups who might wish to build a Community Center or a Daycare or even a

Masque, primarily because of fear. Of course, the city of Ashland, Kentucky once believed a rumor that the local Roman Catholic church had an arsenal of weapons in its basement. Blacks and Hispanics fair no different. As soon as they are spotted by the police, they are more than likely to be involved in a traffic stop, just because. However, they are usually arrested and their vehicle will be searched for illegal drugs. And if they put up the least bit of resistance, guns may be drawn and discharged.

Let's face it, the American justice system is messed up. The American people are scared of their own shadows now. We used to not be this way, we used to have the blatant optimism about the future and we felt we could (and did) achieve anything we put our minds to do. Unfortunately, those days are gone. The new pessimism of the Baby Boomers and the fears they are feeling in their later years, has filtered down into their children (Generation X,) as well as their

grandchildren (the Millennials.) And who
can honestly blame them, once they got to a
point in their careers where they were
making good money and benefits, they
would be downsized from their company,
for whatever reason. This hard lesson does
leave scars, rather deep ones, and its impact
is felt long after the sting has subsided.

Chapter Nine:

We start today with an account of two communities. One is liberal, the other conservative. I want you to guess which is which.

The schools would stress patriotism and respect. And it would be a very rules-based educational system. The houses would be fairly similar. The lawns would be very nicely kept and beautifully green and mowed. The town would be quiet, with lots of churches.

That's town one. Here's town two.

The schools would be based more on experiential kinds of things rather than rote memory. People would prefer older houses with wooden floors rather than wall-to-wall carpeting. They would keep the yards natural - lots of bars and community theaters and foreign films, more of those than churches.

That was easy, right? Conservatives like order. Liberals embrace ambiguity. Now, you may be rolling your eyes or even getting angry at these stereotypes. But we all know there's more than a grain of truth to them. So how did these two towns, referred to as Liberalville (ph) and Conservaton (ph), get this way?

When most of us think about how we came to our political views, we tend to have a straightforward explanation. We use our upbringing and life experiences as the basis for our political beliefs. We imagine that our parents, teachers and friends shape our views on everything, from taxes and the economy to immigration and national security. But what if I told you there is something deeper to those attitudes, drives that shape the music we listen to, the food we eat, the politicians we elect? How the partisan divide in our country might arise not just from our upbringing and lived experiences, but from biology.

On a regular basis, right before an election, someone will share an article with me about how science proves that the brains of liberals are stunted. Or a post on Twitter will say, Republicans are less intelligent than Democrats. These claims obscure something far more interesting and far more accurate. There are genuine psychological differences between liberals and conservatives. Understanding these differences can give us fresh insight into our political conflicts.

When most of us think about how we came to our political views, we have a relatively straightforward explanation that has to do with our upbringing and background. How does that theory go?

And I think we have this sense that those views that our parents have passed along are supplemented by those, you know, from a clergy member or a trusted relative, a close friend. But we sort those through our own view of the world. And we come to a very rational understanding of the world and an understanding of what social policies are best to make the world better.

So, we're going to look in-depth at some of the psychological and brain differences that do exist between liberals and conservatives. But I want to start by looking at how differences between partisans are not limited to politics. These differences show up in many domains that have nothing to do with politics. Republican President George H. W. Bush once spoke about an issue that had bothered him for many years.

GEORGE H. W. BUSH: *I do not like broccoli.*

BUSH: *And I haven't liked it since I was a little kid. And my mother made me eat it. And I'm president of the United States. And I'm not going to eat any more broccoli.*

What do food differences tell us about liberals and conservatives?

Well, we tend to see that there are differences in tastes. Conservatives do like meat and potatoes more. Liberals are more likely to prefer ethnic food. So, you see that. And that, we think, is part of a deeper pattern of conservatives are a little bit fonder of kind of predictability, of standard kinds of things. And liberals are a little bit more willing to experiment. And this comes through in food tastes and a variety of other things.

Here's another example. Researchers once went into the living spaces of people - offices and dorm rooms. And they recorded the items that they saw. What was different about the living and work spaces of liberals and conservatives?

Well, conservatives tended to have lots of things like sports memorabilia, whereas liberals tended to have more experiential things - lots of books, lots of CDs, especially diverse CDs, whereas conservatives were more likely to have things that organized their lives - calendars, clothes baskets. Also, the researchers suggested the liberals' rooms were not quite as tidy or as well-lighted as the conservative rooms and offices.

There's even been some research looking at differences in our preferences for different kinds of pets. I understand Jonathan Haidt and others have explored that liberals and conservatives gravitate to different kinds of dogs.

Different kinds of dogs - it tends to be the case that conservatives prefer purebreds. And liberals will go with mixed-breed dogs. There are some studies that suggest how you view pets - there isn't that much difference in how many have pets. Both liberals and conservatives like to have pets at about equal level. But they might view them somewhat differently. Liberals are a little bit more likely to view them as part of the family rather than, you know, just a pet. So, you have those kinds of very interesting things, not just in pet ownership, but kind of in orientation to the pet.

The patterns that John and others have identified are more than just curious. These patterns suggest that our model of political differences is wrong in an important way. Liberals and conservatives don't just have different political preferences. They have different temperaments. Conservatives don't just care about lower taxes. They also care about whether poetry rhymes.

That's right. Should poetry rhyme? We also ask, you know, are you more comfortable with novels that end with clear resolution, those kinds of things. And, you know, you can start to see a pattern already, I think, in our discussion, that it is the case that liberals are more likely to say, sure, I'm OK with free verse, whereas conservatives say, no, you know, we really think there should be a pattern. Music should come back to a recognizable melody. Poetry should rhyme.

And novels should - should wrap up in a way that we are comfortable with.

To be clear, the differences identifies are averages. So, you can certainly have a Republican who likes free verse and a Democrat who hates jazz. The point of this research isn't to stereotype liberals and conservatives but to show that our political choices flow from deeply ingrained psychological differences. Many of us don't realize how our choices as consumers - the cars we buy, the food we eat, the music we listen to - that these choices inadvertently reveal our political preferences.

So, I'm happy to tell people on Facebook what kind of music I listen to. But I imagine that they wouldn't be able to tell from that whether I was a Democrat or a Republican. I asked John about research that suggests you can tell whether someone's a conservative or a liberal if you know what kind of movies they watch, what kind of food they eat, what kind of vacations they take.

It's very reasonable that people would not resonate with that line of argument because to them, it's not like they say, well, you know, in order to be a good conservative, I need to do this - or in order to be a good liberal. So, you know, they're just being themselves. And I think that's the real message here, is that our political beliefs are part and parcel of our entire being. You know, it's not like they're completely separate. And it's just a natural outgrowth of these larger psychological and even physiological tendencies that we've been talking about.

I want to start with one of the most important differences you and others have identified when it comes to politics. Liberals and conservatives differ when it comes to how they see threats and danger. Here's Wayne LaPierre of the National Rifle Association.

WAYNE LAPIERRE: *We know, in the world that surrounds us, there are terrorists,*

*and there are home invaders, drug cartels,
carjackers, knockout gamers and rapists and
haters and campus killers, airport killers,
shopping mall killers...*

So, you know, you get the sense that if you
listen to this very long, you're scared of
everything. The message that I take from
this is that, you know, you play this to
liberals, and they say, this guy is nuts. You
know, others have told me he's just doing it
because he makes millions of dollars from
the NRA, and he doesn't really believe it.

I think he does. These threats are very real to
him, and we're not going to get anywhere
unless people who don't feel that way
understand that some people do. And
likewise, the Wayne LaPierres of the world
need to understand that for some people,
they just - you know, they don't see the
world as threatening as he does. And they
don't think we need to build our society
around mitigating those threats.

So, you know, when a liberal like Jon Stewart hides behind the desk, partly what he's doing is he's mocking Wayne LaPierre. He's sort of saying, this is ridiculous. It's beyond ridiculous to imagine that all these threats are basically around us. We live in a relatively safe society. And basically, what Jon Stewart is communicating is, you know, what you're saying doesn't make any sense. And what you're saying is, it might not make sense to you. But it makes sense to Wayne LaPierre.

Exactly. You know, one of the favorite things for conservatives to say about liberals is that they just don't get it - meaning that, you know, they don't appreciate that it's a dangerous world. And I think that is absolutely true. But it's not that they don't get it because they're being obtuse or they're not informed. They read about events in the world, and they just don't respond to them in the same way.

And like wise con - liberals, rather, need to recognize that while this may seem silly - and you're right about Jon Stewart mocking this - you know, how can you live your life worried and whatever. But to them, this is very real. And a good citizen is vigilant and is prepared to do battle to protect himself, his family and society from those threats.

What's interesting about both groups here is that there is a very powerful illusion that we have that the rest of the world sees the world the way that we see the world. And if they come to a different conclusion, it must be because they're being deliberately obtuse or somehow deliberately biased, as opposed to the idea that people are actually - they might be seeing the world the same way, but their reactions to world might actually be very different.

Psychologists talk about false consensus. It turns out that if your favorite color is blue, you grossly overstate the percent of the population whose favorite color is blue. So, you know, I think we need to recognize that. We did a study once. There's a substance, androsterone - it turns out that people smell it very differently. It's just because our olfactory systems are structured differently. Some people smell it very favorably. It smells like kind of cookies or incense. Others smell it unfavorably. It'll smell like sweat or even urine. And some don't smell it at all. And it's a genetically based difference. So, we had a bunch of our graduate students smell this. And I remember one fellow, and he smelled it, and it just smelled awful to him. And it didn't smell awful to many of the other graduate students. And he was convinced that this was some kind of psychological trick, that we were trying to, you know, get him to say, well, yeah, it doesn't smell bad. It was one of those studies. When in fact, he just couldn't believe that people were that different in the way they smelled this substance. And I think the same thing applies to political beliefs and to the way we experience threats in the world.

But this idea that, you know, the way that we see, hear, something must be the way everyone else sees it, and there's just this feeling of utter disbelief that other people might not see and hear the world the same way.

So, I do think that's something we need to continue to pound away on - that we really are wired up quite differently.

Let's look at how this plays out when it comes to the subject of immigration. Here is Republican Donald Trump.

PRESIDENT DONALD TRUMP: *They're bringing drugs. They're bringing crime. They're rapists. And some, I assume, are good people.* And then there is the Speaker of the House, Nancy Pelosi.

NANCY PELOSI: *We are constantly reinvigorated by immigrants coming to our*

These are politicians. They might indeed be saying things that are just politically strategic. But how might differences in threat perception shape the way liberals and conservatives in general think about the subject of immigration?

Yeah, I really think - you know, immigration, defense, police, law and order - I think this is really at the core of who we are and at the core of political differences. So, you know, if I am a person like Wayne LaPierre who feels these threats and thinks they're all around us, then it seems to me I would want a set of policies put forward by our government that helped to reduce those threats. And how am I going to do this? I'm going to do it by allowing people to be well-armed. I'm going to do it by spending a lot on defense. I'm going to empower police.

I'm going to have the death penalty. And I'm going to not allow immigrants to come here. Or if they do, they are going to be extremely vetted, as the presidents once said. So, you know, those, I think, to a threat-sensitive mindset, are steps that - you know, they only make sense. They just can't really understand why anybody would be opposed to those kinds of things because this would help us to be a safer place.

Now, there are all kinds of confounding factors when it comes to studying how politicians speak in the actual world, political considerations that are difficult to disentangle from psychological and biological traits. But John and others have studied these differences in experimental settings. John once showed liberals and conservatives positive and negative pictures, and he found they reacted very differently.

A positive picture would be something like a beautiful sunset or somebody enjoying themselves on a ski slope, a happy child. A

negative picture would be things like a
house that had just been leveled by a
hurricane or a guy eating worms or children
who are malnourished. We had people
hooked up to some physiological devices.
The most obvious one is electrodermal
activity or skin conductance, which is a
common way of seeing if somebody is just
having a reaction - having a physiological
arousal to that stimulus. And what we found
is that people do have arousals when they
see these kinds of images because they have
some emotional content. But we tended to
find that liberals were more reactive to the
positive images, and conservatives are more
reactive to the negative images.

In one brain-imaging study that was
conducted, volunteers were shown
disgusting images. And brain activation
from even a single image was actually pretty
good at being able to tell who was liberal
and who was conservative.

That's true. There have been three or four
studies that attempt to see if the brain
activation patterns of liberals and
conservatives is different. And the one that
we did goes back to kind of our favorite
thing, which is to show them these different
kinds of pictures. Actually, we had the most
luck with pictures of mutilations. And you're
right. When we did that, it was very easy to
categorize people, you know, without
knowing anything about them. All we would
look at was the brain scan results. And we
could be incredibly accurate knowing
whether they were liberal or conservative
just on the basis of that. Liberals' brains,
when they looked at mutilation images, were
much more active in a part of the brain
called the S2, somatosensory 2. And this is
part of the brain that will be activated if you
suffer pain. So, if I kick you in the shin,
your somatosensory 2 would be active. But
it's also active if you see pain in others. And
so, if you would see a movie of somebody
stepping on a rusty nail - goes right through

their foot - your somatosensory 2 would be active. And what we saw in these brain scans was that liberals were more likely to have activation in the somatosensory 2 than conservatives. Doesn't mean that conservatives are hard-hearted; it just means that things are happening differently when they see these different images.

Now, you could argue that a lot of this research is correlational. You could also argue that a lot of the patterns that John and others find are consistent with the power of upbringing in shaping political preferences. Here's how. Let's say I'm raised in a conservative home. I learned to be politically conservative from my parents, but my family also influences all kinds of other things about me that have nothing to do with politics. They shape the kind of food I like to eat, the kind of movies I like to watch, the kind of sports I enjoy. By this line of reasoning, the fact that liberals and conservatives are different on all manner of things isn't about biology. It just shows you how your family environment can affect lots of things about you.

There's a really interesting way to separate the effects of biology from the environment. Think about fraternal and identical twins. Identical twins have identical genes. Fraternal twins have similar but not identical genes. If you follow a group of fraternal and identical twins, each twin pair is raised in the same household. Each pair eats the same food, listens to the same conversations, watches the same movies. Now, if you find differences between identical twins as a group and fraternal twins as a group, that suggests that biology, not environment, is the driver. What such studies reveal about political preferences.

We were fortunate to have access to a data set. It's very large, includes thousands and thousands of twin pairs, collected by a guy named Lindon Eaves long ago. It's a fairly dated data set, but it was a valuable one for us because it included lots of information about their political views. And when we subjected these data to the standard twin design approach, we did indeed find that the political views were quite heritable. Although, people oftentimes misread this, our results suggested that maybe 30 or 40 percent of our political views come from genetics. But, you know, that bothered a lot of people, and this was quite a controversial study in political science. Many people didn't like that at all, and they tended to over-interpret those results and make it sound like we were saying that everything was genetic. But, you know, if it's 30 to 40 percent genetic, that obviously leaves, you know, 50, 60, 70 percent that comes from the environment. So, all we're saying is that that genetic component is not zero, but apparently that was enough that some people were upset about that.

And so, you basically, you're able to tell, in some ways, that there is a closer link in the political orientation of identical twins than in the political orientation of fraternal twins. And that tells you that there is some element of the biology, some element of genetics, that is driving political preferences.

Exactly. Now, that's well put. And again, it's nice to compare political views with other kinds of things. Height, for example, turns out to be about 80 percent heritable when you see these, when you subject it to the same kind of design. Personality traits are about 56 percent. Political views: 30 to 40 percent, I would say.

One of the big implications of all of this work, besides just being interesting in itself, is that it helps us, I think, think about the political conflicts we have with fresh insight. And you've made the case that in many ways, the more we are able to see the differences between groups of people as inherent or biological, in some ways, it changes the way we think about those

differences. Talk to me about that idea,
John.

Yes. When other traits have been understood
to be biological - I'm thinking of something
like handedness. You know, we used to
think that if you were left-handed, that was
just because you got into a lazy habit. My
father was left-handed, and the teacher. you
know, this was long ago - would beat him on
the hand with a ruler whenever he wrote
with his left hand, trained him to write with
his right hand. So, we viewed that as a flaw,
as something that need to be driven out. Of
course, now we understand that being left-
handed is very biological. This is something
much deeper than just a lazy habit. Or, of
course, you know the big one today would
be sexual orientation. When people realized
that sexual orientation is indeed
biologically-driven and not something that
they just have decided to do, then people are
much more tolerant of that. So, if it is
possible if perhaps the same thing might

happen with regard to politics. If we realize that our political opponents were not simply being lazy but rather were oriented to the world in a different fashion, that maybe we would be a little bit more tolerant of them, that this is the only way we're going to get anywhere if we at least understand where they're coming from, even if we still might deeply disagree with their conclusions.

What would you say to critics who would say, you know, the argument that psychological traits and biological differences are beneath our deep political conflicts doesn't make sense because we didn't always have this deep divide in our country between liberals and conservatives? There was a time when we had many, many more people in the center. The most liberal Republican was often to the left of the most conservative Democrat. And, you know, there really has been a sorting of the political parties in recent years. What explains this change, especially over the last 20, 30 years?

What I would say to that argument is that I believe we have always had this very same division, this very basic difference between people who are fairly sensitive to threats and think we need to be vigilant and those people who are more into experimentation and trying new things. Ralph Waldo Emerson has a great quote, and I'm sorry I can't give it to you verbatim. But it's basically that the division between those people who are supporters of tradition and those people who are supportive of innovation is very old and has structured the world since time began.

Interesting, right? Not only is the human brain structurally different between liberals and conservatives, but how they structure the worlds they occupy is also different, possibly explaining why conservative choose Accounting, Economics, or Finance or even Engineering as a career choice, while liberals choose subjects such as Art, Music, Psychology, Social Work or even most of the other social sciences as a career choice.

Chapter Ten:

Blue state, red state. Big government, big business. Gay rights, fetal rights. The United States is riven by the politics of extremes. To paraphrase humor columnist Dave Barry, Republicans think of Democrats as godless, unpatriotic, Volvo-driving, France-loving, elitist latte guzzlers, whereas Democrats dismiss Republicans as ignorant, NASCAR-obsessed, gun-fondling religious fanatics. An exaggeration, for sure, but the reality is still pretty stark. Congress is in a perpetual stalemate because of the two parties' inability to find middle ground on practically anything.

According to the experts who study political leanings, liberals and conservatives do not just see things differently. They are different, in their personalities and even their unconscious reactions to the world around them. For example, in a study published in January, a team led by psychologist Michael Dodd and political scientist John Hibbing of the University of Nebraska–Lincoln found that when viewing a collage of photographs, conservatives' eyes unconsciously lingered 15 percent longer on repellent images, such as car wrecks and excrement, suggesting that conservatives are more attuned than liberals to assessing potential threats.

Meanwhile examining the contents of 76 college students' bedrooms, as one group did in a 2008 study, revealed that conservatives possessed more cleaning and organizational items, such as ironing boards and calendars, confirmation that they are orderly and self-disciplined. Liberals owned more books and travel-related memorabilia, which conforms with previous research suggesting that they are open and novelty-seeking.

"These are not superficial differences. They are psychologically deep," says psychologist John Jost of New York University, a coauthor of the bedroom study. "My hunch is that the capacity to organize the political world into left or right may be a part of human nature."

Although conservatives and liberals are fundamentally different, hints are emerging about how to bring them together—or at least help them coexist. In his recent book The Righteous Mind, psychologist Jonathan Haidt of the N.Y.U. Stern School of Business argues that liberals and conservatives need not revile one another as immoral on issues such as birth control, gay marriage or health care reform. Even if these two worldviews clash, they are equally grounded in ethics, he writes. Meanwhile some studies suggest that political views reside on a continuum that is mediated in part by universal human emotions such as fear. Under certain circumstances, everyone can shift closer to the middle—or drift further apart.

Psychologists have found that conservatives are fundamentally more anxious than liberals, which may be why they typically desire stability, structure and clear answers even to complicated questions. Conservatism, apparently, helps to protect people against some of the natural difficulties of living. The fact is we don't live in a completely safe world. Things can and do go wrong. But if I can impose this order on it by my worldview, I can keep my anxiety to a manageable level.

Anxiety is an emotion that waxes and wanes in all of us, and as it swings up or down our political views can shift in its wake. When people feel safe and secure, they become more liberal; when they feel threatened, they become more conservative. Research conducted in the weeks after September 11, 2001, showed that people of all political persuasions became more conservative in the wake of the terrorist attacks. Meanwhile, in a study, found that asking Republicans to imagine that they possessed superpowers and were impermeable to injury made them more liberal. There is some range within which people can be moved.

More practically, instead of trying to change people's emotional state (an effect that is temporary), astute policy makers might be able to phrase their ideas in a way that appeals to different worldviews. In a 2010 paper, found a way to bring conservatives and liberals together on global warming. She and her colleagues wondered whether the impulse to defend the status quo might be driving the conservative pooh-poohing of environmental issues.

In an ingenious experiment, the psychologists reframed climate change not as a challenge to government and industry but as "a threat to the American way of life." After reading a passage that couched environmental action as patriotic, study participants who displayed traits typical of conservatives were much more likely to sign petitions about preventing oil spills and protecting the Arctic National Wildlife Refuge.

Environmentalism may be an ideal place to find common political ground. Conservatives who are religious have this mind-set about being good stewards of the earth, to protect God's creation, and that is very compatible with green energy and conservation and other ideas that are usually classified as liberal. However, in the current political climate, the fossil fuel industry has a grip upon the policy makers and only when there is sufficient damage done or we are forced to make a difficult choice (no, I do not mean climate change,) will we come together from both ends of the political spectrum to solve the problem.

On topics where liberals and conservatives will never see eye to eye, opposing sides can try to cultivate mutual respect. In "The Righteous Mind", Haidt identifies several areas of morality. Liberals, he says, tend to value two of them: caring for people who are vulnerable and fairness, which for liberals tends to mean sharing resources equally. Conservatives care about those things, too, but for them fairness means proportionality—that people should get what they deserve based on the amount of effort they

have put in. Conservatives also emphasize loyalty and authority, values helpful for maintaining a stable society.

In a 2009 study Haidt and two of his colleagues presented more than 8,000 people with a series of hypothetical actions. Among them: kick a dog in the head; discard a box of ballots to help your candidate win; publicly bet against a favorite sports team; curse your parents to their faces; and receive a blood transfusion from a child molester. Participants had to say whether they would do these deeds for money and, if so, for how much—$10? $1,000? $100,000? More? Liberals were reluctant to harm a living thing or act unfairly, even for $1 million, but they were willing to betray group loyalty, disrespect authority or do something disgusting, such as eating their own dog after it dies, for cash. Conservatives said they were less willing to compromise on any of the moral categories.

Haidt has a message for both sides. He wants the left to acknowledge that the right's emphasis on laws, institutions, customs and religion is valuable. Conservatives recognize that democracy is a huge achievement and that maintaining the social order requires imposing constraints on people. Liberal values, on the other hand, also serve important roles: ensuring that the rights of weaker members of society are respected; limiting the harmful effects, such as pollution, that corporations sometimes pass on to others; and fostering innovation by supporting diverse ideas and ways of life.

Haidt is not out to change people's deepest moral beliefs. Yet he thinks that if people could see that those, they disagree with are not immoral but simply emphasizing different moral principles, some of the antagonism would subside. There is something to be said which finds value in conservative tenets that which used to reject reflexively: "It's yin and yang. Both sides see different threats; both sides are wise to different virtues."

It goes without saying that there are very different thought processes going on in the heads of Trump supporters versus Bernie ones, for example. Many might argue that political views are largely shaped by our environments, but it turns out that our neurobiology may significantly contribute to whether we think like Reds or Blues.

Back in 2013, a team of political scientists and neuroscientists got together to study how liberals and conservatives use different parts of the brain when making risky decisions. Their findings suggest that these brain regions can be used to predict which political party an individual prefers, and that being a Republican or Democrat truly does have an influence on how the brain functions.

The researchers looked into a previous study that measured the brain activity of volunteers playing a gambling game, but they separated the data to compare Democrats and Republicans.

Interestingly, the opposite groups didn't differ in the risks they took, but there were striking differences in the brain activities that lit up during the decision-making process. The Democrats showed significantly greater activity in the left insula, a region associated with emotional processing as well as social and self-awareness, while the Republicans showed significantly greater activity in the right amygdala, a region that plays a role in the body's fight-or-flight system.

This data provides evidence that Democrats and Republicans use different cognitive processes when they think about risk. In fact, the researchers say that the brain activity in these two regions alone could predict whether a person is a Democrat or a Republican with 82.9 percent accuracy, more accurate than using a model based on the political affiliations of an individual's parents, which is only accurate about 69.5 percent of the time.

Other research looked at the psychological differences between Republicans and Democrats, finding fundamental differences between things like morals and fears.

"Conservatism, apparently, helps to protect people against some of the natural difficulties of living," says social psychologist Paul Nail of the University of Central Arkansas. "The fact is we don't live in a completely safe world. Things can and do go wrong. But if I can impose this order on it by my worldview, I can keep my anxiety to a manageable level."

According to Nail's research, people of all political persuasions became more conservative in the weeks after September 11, 2001, showing that fear can play a role in driving Republican views.

Interestingly, in another experiment, psychologists reframed climate change as "a threat to the American way of life" and talked up environmental actions as patriotic. The findings showed that the study volunteers who displayed typical conservative traits were much more likely to sign petitions about preventing oil spills and protecting the Arctic National Wildlife Refuge after the issue was spun in such a way.

In a highly competitive world as conservatives see it, success is interpreted as the result of a combination of talent and hard work.

For this reason, they are opposed to the redistributive processes that characterize welfare states. They also reject progressive taxation under which the high earners pay much higher rates, effectively subsidizing poorer segments of the population who earn less.

Whereas liberals see the poor and destitute as largely being victims of misfortune, such as the unlucky fate of being born to poor minority parents, conservatives emphasize the role of personal defects, such as drug dependency, and unwillingness to work.

These differing perspectives generate very different views of inequality. Liberals see it as a social problem that government must relieve. Conservatives are more comfortable with inequality and accept the Biblical assertion that the poor will always be among us.

Yin and Yang, balance. You see each side is needed in order for our political system to function properly. Each side keeps the other side in check, keeping it either center-right or center-left. This notion of the extremes seizing control of either political viewpoint, is a very scary prospect, indeed. It is like in today's political climate, the right has been seized by some the most extreme elements of the movement, driving out more moderate voices. Running almost on an exclusive platform of God (prayer needs to be put back in the public school and square, because we are a Christian nation,) Guns (the right to keep and bear arms shall not be infringed, even towards the chronically mentally or people who have committed domestic violence,) and Gays (recognition of the LGBTQIA+ community is an abomination towards GOD and recognition of same-sex marriage violates the sanctity of my fourth marriage.) let's include in that platform that the Muslims are coming into this country in order to instill Sharia Law on us all and if they can't do that, they'll kill us all. Now that you have read these words, don't they sound a bit foolish and full of fear?

Conclusion:

In conclusion, all of the research and the various studies have shown that the structure of a liberal brain and a conservative brain is structurally different, partially by family upbringing and partially from the environment. Now this does not mean that the intelligence of a conservative is somehow less than that of a liberal, they are just speaking to the opposite of one another. One is more into concrete reasoning, while the other is of more abstract thinking. Yes, the whole right versus left brain argument comes into play here.

But there are topics where both liberals and conservatives can find common ground. As mentioned in a previous chapter, the environment would be an excellent starting point. Since most conservatives identify as evangelical Christians, one of God's commandments to man was that he was supposed to be a good steward of the earth, in order words, take care of the planet. And most liberals are already involved in the environmental movement, it would not be too far a stretch for each side to move towards the middle and build a consensus.

Now, this business of "owning the libs," is just plain foolish and as evidenced by quite a few conservative's behavior during this COVID-19 pandemic, the business of "owning the libs," caused a great many who failed to believe science, failed to social distance and failed to wear face masks, to fall ill, your loved ones to fall ill, or worse yet cost someone you may or may not know their lives. C'mon folks, we are all adults here. By ignoring the medical experts, you are not only risking your own lives, but possibly the lives of your children and grandchildren, (and I am a grandfather as well, and I don't know anyone who wouldn't do anything for their grandchildren.) And they have found that children can not only contract, get sick and even die from COVID-19, but they can be asymptomatic carriers as well. So, all this talk about reopening schools is a sign of sheer refusal to listen to science. As a matter of fact, one school in Georgia, whose crowded hallways with very few students went viral, two weeks later with over 1000 students testing positive for COVID-19.

And it's not just Georgia, a majority of the states have shown a spike in COVID cases. And this is still part of the first wave. At this moment in time, there is no vaccine, no magic bullet, wishing it away will not get us through it. Only time and patience will. I know, we live in the age of instant gratification, and the majority of the American population has the patience and attention span of a gnat. We want this over and we want it over yesterday, so we can get back to life the way it used to be. Believe me, I'm right there with you. But I also realize that a.) it's not going to be over in the foreseeable future; B.) Life as we know it is not going to return back to any semblance of pre-pandemic; and C.) No amount of wishing, wishful thinking or magical thinking is going to make this pandemic go away. So why am I talking about the pandemic, this is just the most recent example of how differently conservatives and liberals think. I could list a dozen or more scenarios where this has played out over the past twenty years of so. One group thinks is "macho," not to wear masks, while the other attempts to follow all the protocols necessary to stay alive.

Some conservatives argue that they it is an impediment upon their rights to wear a mask. Okay, we can follow that argument. But what they fail to take into account, and this is a prime example of two-dimensional thinking, is that their rights extend no further than the tip of their nose, then they start infringing upon other people's rights.

On a surface level, it's obvious that Republicans and Democrats are different in many ways, but it's intriguing to delve into the psychology and neuroscience of these differences, however, Donald Trump's brain may always remain a bit of a scientific mystery, in my opinion…

Works Cited:

Baker-Brown, G., Ballard, E. J., Bluck, S., de Vries, B., Suedfeld, P., & Tetlock, P. E. (1992). The conceptual/integrative complexity scoring manual. In C. P. Smith (Ed.), Motivation and personality: Handbook of thematic content analysis (pp.

605–611). Cambridge, UK: Cambridge University Press.

Brandt, M. J., Reyna, C., Chambers, J. R., Crawford, J. T., & Wetherell, G. (2014). The Ideological-Conflict Hypothesis: Intolerance among both liberals and conservatives. Current Directions in Psychological Science, 23, 27–34. doi: 10.1177/0963721413510932

Brundidge, J., Reid, S. A., Choi, S., & Muddiman, A. (2014). The "deliberative digital divide:" Opinion leadership and integrative complexity in the U.S. political blogosphere. Political Psychology. doi:10.1111/pops.12201

Conway, L. G., III, & Conway, K. R. (2011). The terrorist rhetorical style and its consequences for understanding terrorist violence. Dynamics of Asymmetric Conflict, 4, 175–192.

Conway, L. G., III, Conway, K. R., Gornick, L. J., & Houck, S. C. (2014). Automated integrative complexity. Political Psychology, 35, 603–624.

Conway, L. G. III, Dodds, D., Hands Towgood, K., McClure, S, & Olson, J. (2011). The biological roots of complex thinking: Are heritable attitudes more complex? Journal of Personality, 79, 101–134.

Conway, L.G., III, & Gornick, L. J. (2011). Cognitive complexity. In D. Christie (Ed.), The encyclopedia of peace psychology (pp. 849–853). Hoboken, NJ: Wiley-Blackwell.

Conway, L. G., III, Gornick, L. J., Burfiend, C., Mandella, P., Kuenzli, A., Houck, S. C., & Fullerton, D. T. (2012). Does simple rhetoric win elections? An integrative complexity analysis of U.S. presidential campaigns. Political Psychology, 33, 599–618.

Conway, L. G., III, Schaller, M., Tweed, R. G., & Hallett, D. (2001). The complexity of thinking across cultures: Interactions between culture and situational context. Social Cognition, 19, 230–253.

Conway, L. G., III, Suedfeld, P., & Clements, S. M. (2003). Beyond the American reaction: Integrative complexity of Middle Eastern leaders during the 9/11 crisis. Psicologia Politica, 27, 93–103.

Conway, L. G., III, Suedfeld, P., & Tetlock, P. E. (2001). Integrative complexity and political decisions that lead to war or peace. In D. J. Christie (Ed.), Peace, conflict, and violence: Peace psychology for the 21st century (pp. 66–75). Upper Saddle River, NJ: Prentice Hall/Pearson Education.

Conway, L. G., III, Thoemmes, F., Allison, A. M., Towgood, K. H., Wagner, M. J., Davey, K., et al. (2008). Two ways to be complex and why they matter: Implications for attitude strength and lying. Journal of Personality and Social Psychology, 95(5), 1029–1044.

Crawford, J. T. (2012). The ideologically objectionable premise model: Predicting biased political judgments on the left and right. Journal of Experimental Social Psychology, 48, 138–151.

Dasen, P. R. (1975). Concrete operational development in three cultures. Journal of Cross-Cultural Psychology, 6, 156–172.

Duarte, J. L., Crawford, J. T., Stern, C., Haidt, J., Jussim, L., & Tetlock, P. E. (in press). Political diversity will improve social psychological science. Behavioral and Brain Sciences.

Eaves, L. J., Eysenck, H. J., & Martin, N. G. (1989). Genes, culture, and personality: An empirical approach. London, UK: Academic Press.

Fazio, R. H., Jackson, J. R., Dunton, B. C., & Williams, C. J. (1995). Variability in automatic activation as an unobtrusive measure of racial attitudes: A bona fide pipeline? Journal of Personality and Social Psychology, 69, 1013– 1027.

Federico, C. M., Deason, G., & Fisher, E. L. (2012). Ideological asymmetry in the relationship between epistemic motivation and political attitudes. Journal of Personality and Social Psychology. doi:10.1037/a0029063

Graham, J., Haidt, J., & Nosek, B. (2009). Liberals and conservatives rely on different sets of moral foundations. Journal of Personality and Social Psychology, 96, 1029–1046.

Houck, S. C., Conway, L. G., III, & Gornick, L. J. (2014). Automated integrative complexity: Current challenges and future directions. Political Psychology, 35(5), 647– 659.

Harvey, O. J., Hunt, D. E., & Schroder, H. M. (1961). Conceptual systems and personality organization. Oxford, UK: Wiley.

Joseph, C. M., Graham, J., & Haidt, J. (2009). The end of equipotentiality: A moral foundations approach to ideology attitude links and cognitive complexity. Psychological Inquiry, 20, 172–176.

Jost, T., Glaser, J., Kruglanski, A. W., & Sulloway, F. J. (2003). Political conservatism as motivated social cognition. Psychological Bulletin 129(3), 339–375.

Judd, C. M., & Lusk, C. M. (1984). Knowledge structures and evaluative judgments: Effects of structural variables on judgmental extremity. Journal of Personality and Social Psychology, 46, 1193–1207. 20 Conway et al.

Lavallee, L., & Suedfeld, P. (1997). Conflict in Clayoquot Sound: Using thematic content analysis to understand psychological aspects of environmental controversy. Canadian Journal of Behavioral Science, 29, 194–209.

Liht, J., Conway, L. G. III, Savage, S., White, W., O'Neill, K. A. (2011). Religious fundamentalism: An empirically derived construct and measurement scale. Archive for the Psychology of Religion, 33, 299–323.

Martin, N. G., Eaves, L.J., Heath. A. R., Jardine, R., Feingold, L. M., & Eysenck, H. J. (1986). Transmission of social attitudes. Proceedings of the National Academy of Science, 83, 4364–4368.

Neuberg, S. L., & Newsom, J. T. (1993). Personal need for structure: Individual differences in the desire for simpler structure. Journal of Personality and Social Psychology, 65, 113–131.

Olson, J. M., Vernon, P.A., Harris, J., & Jang, K. L. (2001). The heritability of attitudes: A study of twins. Journal of Personality and Social Psychology. 80, 845–860.

Pancer, S. M., Jackson, L. M., Hunsberger, B., Pratt, M. W., et al. (1995). Religious orthodoxy and the complexity of thought about religious and nonreligious issues. Journal of Personality, 63, 213–232.

Ray, J. J. (1970). The development and validation of a balanced dogmatism scale. Australian Journal of Psychology, 22, 253–260.

Rokeach, M. (1960). The open and closed mind: Investigations into the nature of belief systems and personality systems. New York, NY: Basic Books.

Schroder, H. M., Driver, M. J., & Streufert, S. (1965). Information processing systems in individuals and groups. New York, NY: Holt, Rinehart, & Winston.

Sibley, C. G., & Duckitt, J. (2008). Personality and prejudice: A meta-analysis and theoretical review. Personality and Social Psychology Review, 12, 248–279.

Sibley, C. G., Osborne, D., & Duckitt, J. (2012). Personality and political orientation: meta-analysis and test of a threat constraint model. Journal of Research in Personality, 46, 664–677.

Sidanius, J. (1984). Political interest, political information search, and ideological homogeneity as a function of sociopolitical ideology: A tale of three theories. Human Relations, 37, 811–828.

Simons, H. W. (1968). Dogmatism scales and leftist bias. Speech Monographs, 35, 149–153.

Simonton, D. K. (2006). Presidential IQ, openness, intellectual brilliance, and leadership: Estimates and correlations for 42 U.S. chief executives. Political Psychology, 27, 511–526.

Suedfeld, P. (2000). Domain-related variation in integrative complexity: A measure of political importance and responsiveness? Clinton, Gingrich, Gorbachev, and various Canadian political leaders. In O. Feldman & C. De Landtsheer (Eds.), Beyond public speech and symbols: Explorations in the rhetoric of politicians and the media (pp. 17–34). Westport, CT: Praeger.

Suedfeld, P., & Bluck, S. (1988). Changes in integrative complexity prior to surprise attacks. Journal of Conflict Resolution, 26, 626–635.

Suedfeld, P., Bluck, S., & Ballard, E. J. (1994). The effects of emotional involvement and psychological distance on integrative complexity. Journal of Applied Social Psychology, 24, 443–452.

Suedfeld, P., Bluck, S., Loewen, L., & Elkins, D. (1994). Sociopolitical values and integrative complexity of members of student political groups. Canadian Journal of Behavioral Science, 26, 121–141.

Suedfeld, P., Bochner, S., & Wnek, D. (1972). Helper-sufferer similarity and specific request for help: Bystander intervention during a peace demonstration. Journal of Applied Social Psychology, 2, 17–23.

Suedfeld, P., & Leighton, D. C. (2002). Early communications in the war against terrorism: An integrative complexity analysis. Political Psychology, 23, 585–599.

Suedfeld, P., & Rank, A. D. (1976). Revolutionary leaders: Long-term success as a function of changes in conceptual complexity. Journal of Personality and Social Psychology, 34, 169–178.

Suedfeld, P., Steel, G. D., & Schmidt, P. W. (1994). Political ideology and attitudes toward censorship. Journal of Applied Social Psychology, 24, 765–781.

Suedfeld, P., & Streufert, S. (1966). Information search as a function of conceptual and environmental complexity. Psychonomic Science, 4(10), 351–352.

Suedfeld, P., & Tetlock, P. (1976). Integrative complexity of communications in international crises. Journal of Conflict Resolution, 21(1), 169–184.

Suedfeld, P., Tetlock, P., & Streufert, S. (1992). Conceptual/integrative complexity. In C. P. Smith (Ed.), Motivation and personality: Handbook of thematic content analysis (pp. 393–400). Cambridge, MA: Cambridge University Press.

Suedfeld, P., & Wallbaum, A. B. C. (1992). Modifying integrative complexity in political thought: Value conflict and audience disagreement. International Journal of Psychology, 26, 19–36.

Tetlock, P. E. (1984). Cognitive style and political belief systems in the British House of Commons. Journal of Personality and Social Psychology, 46, 365–375. Ideology and Complexity 21

Tetlock, P. E. (1986). A value pluralism model of ideological reasoning. Journal of Personality and Social Psychology, 50, 819–827.

Tetlock, P. E., & Boettger, R. (1989). Cognitive and rhetorical styles of traditionalist and reformist Soviet politicians: A content analysis study. Political Psychology, 10, 209–232.

Tetlock, P. E., Emlen Metz, S., Scott, S. E., & Suedfeld, P. (2014). Integrative complexity coding raises integratively complex issues. Political Psychology, 35, 625–634.

Tetlock, P. E., Peterson, R. & Lerner, J. (1996). Revising the value pluralism model: Incorporating social content and context postulates. In C. Seligman, J. Olson, & M. Zanna (Eds.), Values: The Ontario symposium on personality and social psychology (Vol. 8, pp. 25–51). Hillsdale, NJ: Lawrence Erlbaum.

Thoemmes, F. J., & Conway, L. G., III. (2007). Integrative complexity of 41 U.S. presidents. Political Psychology, 28, 193–226.

Van Hiel, A., & Mervielde, I. (2003). The measurement of cognitive complexity and its relationship with political extremism. Political Psychology, 24(4), 781–801.

Van Hiel, A., Onraet, E., & De Pauw, S. (2010). The relationship between social-cultural attitudes and behavioral measures of cognitive style: A meta-analytic integration of studies. Journal of Personality, 78, 1765–1800.

Webster, D. M., & Kruglanski, A. W. (1994). Individual differences in need for cognitive closure. Journal of Personality and Social Psychology, 67, 1049–1062.

Jost, John T.; Amodio, David M. (13 November 2011). "Political ideology as motivated social cognition: Behavioral and neuroscientific evidence" (PDF). Motivation and Emotion. 36 (1): 55–64. doi:10.1007/s11031-011-9260-7.

Buchen, Lizzie (2012-10-25). "Biology and ideology: The anatomy of politics". Nature. 490 (7421): 466–468. doi:10.1038/490466a. PMID 23099382.

R. Kanai; et al. (2011-04-05). "Political Orientations Are Correlated with Brain

Structure in Young Adults". Curr Biol. 21 (8): 677–80. doi:10.1016/j.cub.2011.03.017. PMC 3092984. PMID 21474316.

Liberal vs. Conservative: Does the Difference Lie in the Brain? – TIME Healthland

Carlson, Neil R. (12 January 2012). Physiology of Behavior. Pearson. p. 364. ISBN 978-0205239399.

Bzdok D, Langner R, Caspers S, Kurth F, Habel U, Zilles K, Laird A, Eickhoff SB (January 2011). "ALE meta-analysis on facial judgments of trustworthiness and attractiveness". Brain Structure & Function. 215 (3–4): 209–23. doi:10.1007/s00429-010-0287-4. PMC 4020344. PMID 20978908.

Kennedy DP, Gläscher J, Tyszka JM, Adolphs R (October 2009). "Personal space regulation by the human amygdala". Nature Neuroscience. 12 (10): 1226–7.

doi:10.1038/nn.2381. PMC 2753689. PMID 19718035.

Bickart KC, Wright CI, Dautoff RJ, Dickerson BC, Barrett LF (February 2011). "Amygdala volume and social network size in humans". Nature Neuroscience. 14 (2): 163–4. doi:10.1038/nn.2724. PMC 3079404. PMID 21186358.

Szalavitz, Maia (28 December 2010). "How to Win Friends: Have a Big Amygdala?". Time. Archived from the original on 17 July 2011. Retrieved 30 December 2010.

T.L. Brink. (2008) Psychology: A Student Friendly Approach. "Unit 4: The Nervous System." pp 61 "Archived copy" (PDF). Archived (PDF) from the original on 3 March 2016. Retrieved 7 February 2016.

Feinstein JS, Adolphs R, Damasio A, Tranel D (January 2011). "The human amygdala and the induction and experience of fear". Current Biology. 21 (1): 34–8.

doi:10.1016/j.cub.2010.11.042. PMC 3030206. PMID 21167712.

Staut CC, Naidich TP (April 1998). "Urbach-Wiethe disease (Lipoid proteinosis)". Pediatric Neurosurgery. 28 (4): 212–4. doi:10.1159/000028653. PMID 9732251. S2CID 46862405.

Y. Inbar; et al. (2008). "Conservatives are more easily disgusted than liberals" (PDF). Cognition and Emotion. 23 (4): 714–725. CiteSeerX 10.1.1.372.3053. doi:10.1080/02699930802110007.

Sanfey AG, Rilling JK, Aronson JA, Nystrom LE, Cohen JD (June 2003). "The neural basis of economic decision-making in the Ultimatum Game". Science. 300 (5626): 1755–8. Bibcode:2003Sci...300.1755S. doi:10.1126/science.1082976. PMID 12805551. S2CID 7111382.

B. Wicker; et al. (2003). "Both of us disgusted in My insula: The common neural basis of seeing and feeling disgust" (PDF).

Neuron. 40 (3): 655–664.
doi:10.1016/s0896-6273(03)00679-2. PMID
14642287.

Wright P, He G, Shapira NA, Goodman
WK, Liu Y (October 2004). "Disgust and
the insula: fMRI responses to pictures of
mutilation and contamination".
NeuroReport. 15 (15): 2347–51.
doi:10.1097/00001756-200410250-00009.
PMID 15640753.

Lane RD, Reiman EM, Axelrod B, Yun LS,
Holmes A, Schwartz GE (July 1998).
"Neural correlates of levels of emotional
awareness. Evidence of an interaction
between emotion and attention in the
anterior cingulate cortex". Journal of
Cognitive Neuroscience. 10 (4): 525–35.
doi:10.1162/089892998562924. PMID
9712681.

Price DD (June 2000). "Psychological and
neural mechanisms of the affective
dimension of pain". Science. 288 (5472):

1769–72. Bibcode:2000Sci...288.1769P. doi:10.1126/science.288.5472.1769. PMID 10846154. S2CID 15250446.

H. Critchley; et al. (2001). "Neural activity in the human brain relating to uncertainty and arousal during anticipation". Neuron. 29 (2): 537–545. doi:10.1016/s0896-6273(01)00225-2. hdl:21.11116/0000-0001-A313-1. PMID 11239442.

Bush G, Luu P, Posner MI (June 2000). "Cognitive and emotional influences in anterior cingulate cortex". Trends in Cognitive Sciences. 4 (6): 215–222. doi:10.1016/S1364-6613(00)01483-2. PMID 10827444.

"Politics on the Brain: Scans Show Whether You Lean Left or Right". LiveScience. Retrieved September 25, 2012.

Kattalia, Kathryn (April 8, 2011). "The liberal brain? Scans show liberals and conservatives have different brain

structures". New York Daily News.
Retrieved September 25, 2012.

 J. Vigil; et al. (2010). "Political leanings
vary with facial expression processing and
psychosocial functioning". Group Processes
& Intergroup Relations. 13 (5): 547–558.
doi:10.1177/1368430209356930.

 J. Jost; et al. (2006). "The end of the end of
ideology" (PDF). American Psychologist. 61
(7): 651–670. doi:10.1037/0003-
066x.61.7.651. PMID 17032067.

 J. Jost; et al. (2003). "Political conservatism
as motivated social cognition" (PDF).
Psychological Bulletin. 129 (3): 339–375.
doi:10.1037/0033-2909.129.3.339. PMID
12784934.

 David M Amodio, John T Jost, Sarah L
Master & Cindy M Yee, Neurocognitive
correlates of liberalism and conservatism,
Nature Neuroscience. Cited by 69 other
studies

"Brains of Liberals, Conservatives May Work Differently". Psych Central. 2007-10-20. Archived from the original on 2016-10-13.

"Study finds left-wing brain, right-wing brain". Los Angeles Times. 2007-09-10.

Elad-Strenger, Julia, Jutta Proch, and Thomas Kessler. "Is Disgust a "Conservative" Emotion?" Personality and Social Psychology Bulletin (2019): 0146167219880191.

Zamboni G, Gozzi M, Krueger F, Duhamel JR, Sirigu A, Grafman J (2009). "Individualism, conservatism, and radicalism as criteria for processing political beliefs: a parametric fMRI study". Social Neuroscience. 4 (5): 367–83. doi:10.1080/17470910902860308. PMID 19562629. Zamboni G, Gozzi M, Krueger F, Duhamel JR, Sirigu A, Jordan Grafman. National Institutes of Health, Bethesda, MD, USA

Kristine Knudson; et al. (March 2006). "Politics on the Brain: An fMRI Investigation". Soc Neurosci. 1 (1): 25–40. doi:10.1080/17470910600670603. PMC 1828689. PMID 17372621.

Aue T, Lavelle LA, Cacioppo JT (July 2009). "Great expectations: what can fMRI research tell us about psychological phenomena?" (PDF). International Journal of Psychophysiology. 73 (1): 10–6. doi:10.1016/j.ijpsycho.2008.12.017. PMID 19232374.

Raj, A; van Oudenaarden, A (2008). "Nature, nurture, or chance: stochastic gene expression and its consequences". Cell. 135 (2): 216–26. doi:10.1016/j.cell.2008.09.050. PMC 3118044. PMID 18957198.

Martin, Nicholas; Boomsma, Dorret; Machin, Geoffrey (17 December 1997). "A twin-pronged attack on complex traits" (PDF). Nature Genetics. 17 (4): 387–92. doi:10.1038/ng1297-387.

Beckwith, Jon; Morris, Corey A. (December 2008). "Twin Studies of Political Behavior: Untenable Assumptions?". Perspectives on Politics. 6 (4): 785–91. doi:10.1017/S1537592708081917.

Fiske, Susan T.; Gilbert, Daniel T.; Lindzey, Gardner (15 February 2010). Handbook of Social Psychology (PDF) (5th ed.). John Wiley & Sons. p. 372.

Carey, Benedict (June 21, 2005). "Some Politics May Be Etched in the Genes". The New York Times. Retrieved September 25, 2012.

Alford, J. R.; Funk, C. L.; Hibbing, J. R. (2005). "Are Political Orientations Genetically Transmitted?". American Political Science Review. 99 (2): 153–167. CiteSeerX 10.1.1.622.476. doi:10.1017/S0003055405051579.

Hatemi, P. K.; Gillespie, N. A.; Eaves, L. J.; Maher, B. S.; Webb, B. T.; Heath, A. C.; Medland, S. E.; Smyth, D. C.; Beeby, H. N.; Gordon, S. D.; Montgomery, G. W.; Zhu, G.; Byrne, E. M.; Martin, N. G. (2011). "A Genome-Wide Analysis of Liberal and Conservative Political Attitudes". The Journal of Politics. 73: 271–285. CiteSeerX 10.1.1.662.2987. doi:10.1017/S0022381610001015.

Michael Bang Petersen. The evolutionary psychology of Mass Politics. In Roberts, S. C. (2011). Roberts, S. Craig (ed.). Applied Evolutionary Psychology. Oxford University Press. doi:10.1093/acprof:oso/9780199586073.001.0001. ISBN 9780199586073.

"Strong men more likely to vote Conservative". The Telegraph. April 11, 2012. Retrieved September 25, 2012.

Dean, T. (2012). "Evolution and Moral Diversity". The Baltic International Yearbook of Cognition, Logic and Communication. 7. doi:10.4148/biyclc.v7i0.1775

Jost JT, Glaser J, Kruglanski AW, Sulloway FJ (2003) Political conservatism as motivated social cognition. Psychological Bulletin 129: 339–375. [PubMed] [Google Scholar]

Kam CD, Simas EN (2010) Risk orientations and policy frames. The Journal of Politics 72: 381–396. [Google Scholar]

Jost JT (2006) The end of the end of ideology. Am Psychol 61: 651–670. [PubMed] [Google Scholar]

Converse P (1964) The Nature of Belief Systems in Mass Publics. In: Apter D, editor. Ideology and Discontent. New York: Free Press. 206–261.

Oxley DR, Smith KB, Alford JR, Hibbing MV, Miller JL, et al. (2008) Political attitudes vary with physiological traits. Science 321: 1667–1670. [PubMed] [Google Scholar]

Amodio DM, Jost JT, Master SL, Yee CM (2007) Neurocognitive correlates of liberalism and conservatism. Nat Neurosci 10: 1246–1247. [PubMed] [Google Scholar]

Fellows LK (2004) The cognitive neuroscience of human decision making: a review and conceptual framework. Behav Cogn Neurosci Rev 3: 159–172. [PubMed] [Google Scholar]

Schonberg T, Fox CR, Poldrack RA (2011) Mind the gap: bridging economic and naturalistic risk-taking with cognitive neuroscience. Trends Cogn Sci 15: 11–19. [PMC free article] [PubMed] [Google Scholar]

Slovic P (2000) The perception of risk. London; Sterling, VA: Earthscan Publications. xxxvii, 473 p. p.

Bechara A (2001) Neurobiology of decision-making: risk and reward. Semin Clin Neuropsychiatry 6: 205–216. [PubMed] [Google Scholar]

Knutson B, Greer SM (2008) Anticipatory affect: neural correlates and consequences for choice. Philosophical Transactions of the Royal Society B: Biological Sciences 363: 3771–3786. [PMC free article] [PubMed] [Google Scholar]

Vorhold V (2008) The neuronal substrate of risky choice: an insight into the contributions of neuroimaging to the understanding of theories on decision making under risk. Ann N Y Acad Sci 1128: 41–52. [PubMed] [Google Scholar]

Lang PJ, Cuthbert BN (1984) Affective information processing and the assessment of anxiety. J Behav Assess 6: 369–395. [PubMed] [Google Scholar]

Mogg K, Mathews A, Weinman J (1989) Selective processing of threat cues in anxiety states: a replication. Behav Res Ther 27: 317–323. [PubMed] [Google Scholar]

Kanai R, Feilden T, Firth C, Rees G (2011) Political Orientations Are Correlated with Brain Structure in Young Adults. Current biology 21: 677–680. [PMC free article] [PubMed] [Google Scholar]

Bechara A, Damasio H, Damasio AR (2003) Role of the amygdala in decision-making. Amygdala in Brain Function: Basic and Clinical Approaches 985: 356–369. [PubMed] [Google Scholar]

Levine DS (2009) Brain pathways for cognitive-emotional decision making in the human animal. Neural Networks 22: 286–293. [PubMed] [Google Scholar]

Morrison SE, Salzman CD (2010) Re-valuing the amygdala. Curr Opin Neurobiol 20: 221–230. [PMC free article] [PubMed] [Google Scholar]

Craig ADB (2011) Significance of the insula for the evolution of human awareness of feelings from the body. Ann N Y Acad Sci 1225: 72–82. [PubMed] [Google Scholar]

Critchley HD (2005) Neural mechanisms of autonomic, affective, and cognitive integration. J Comp Neurol 493: 154–166. [PubMed] [Google Scholar]

Botvinick MM (2007) Conflict monitoring and decision making: reconciling two perspectives on anterior cingulate function. Cogn Affect Behav Neurosci 7: 356–366. [PubMed] [Google Scholar]

Botvinick MM, Cohen JD, Carter CS (2004) Conflict monitoring and anterior cingulate cortex: an update. Trends Cogn Sci 8: 539–546. [PubMed] [Google Scholar]

Abramowitz A, Saunders K (1998) Ideological Realignment in the U.S. Electorate. Journal of Politics 60: 634–652. [Google Scholar]

Abramowitz AI, Saunders KL (2008) Is polarization a myth? Journal of Politics 70: 542–555. [Google Scholar]

Jacobson GC (2004) Partisan and Ideological Polarization in the California Electorate. State Politics & Policy Quarterly 4: 113–139. [Google Scholar]

Paulus MP, Rogalsky C, Simmons A, Feinstein JS, Stein MB (2003) Increased activation in the right insula during risk-taking decision making is related to harm avoidance and neuroticism. Neuroimage 19: 1439–1448. [PubMed] [Google Scholar]

Arce E, Miller DA, Feinstein JS, Stein MB, Paulus MP (2006) Lorazepam dose-dependently decreases risk-taking related activation in limbic areas. Psychopharmacology 189: 105–116. [PMC free article] [PubMed] [Google Scholar]

Paulus MP, Hozack N, Frank L, Brown GG, Schuckit MA (2003) Decision making by methamphetamine-dependent subjects is associated with error-rate-independent decrease in prefrontal and parietal activation. Biol Psychiatry 53: 65–74. [PubMed] [Google Scholar]

Lieberman M, Schreiber D, Ochsner K (2003) Is Political Sophistication Like Learning to Ride a Bicycle? How Cognitive Neuroscience Can Inform Research on Political Thinking. Political Psychology 24: 681–704. [Google Scholar]

Sarinopoulos I, Grupe DW, Mackiewicz KL, Herrington JD, Lor M, et al. (2010) Uncertainty during anticipation modulates neural responses to aversion in human insula and amygdala. Cereb Cortex 20: 929–940. [PMC free article] [PubMed] [Google Scholar]

Gallagher M, Holland PC (1994) The amygdala complex: multiple roles in associative learning and attention. Proceedings of the National Academy of Sciences of the United States of America 91: 11771–11776. [PMC free article] [PubMed] [Google Scholar]

Buchel C, Morris J, Dolan RJ, Friston KJ (1998) Brain systems mediating aversive conditioning: an event-related fMRI study. Neuron 20: 947–957. [PubMed] [Google Scholar]

LeDoux JE (1992) Brain mechanisms of emotion and emotional learning. Curr Opin Neurobiol 2: 191–197. [PubMed] [Google Scholar]

Breiter HC, Rosen BR (1999) Functional magnetic resonance imaging of brain reward circuitry in the human. Ann N Y Acad Sci 877: 523–547. [PubMed] [Google Scholar]

Canli T, Zhao Z, Brewer J, Gabrieli JD, Cahill L (2000) Event-related activation in the human amygdala associates with later memory for individual emotional experience. J Neurosci 20: RC99. [PMC free article] [PubMed] [Google Scholar]

Ernst M, Bolla K, Mouratidis M, Contoreggi C, Matochik JA, et al. (2002) Decision-making in a risk-taking task: a PET study. Neuropsychopharmacology 26: 682–691. [PubMed] [Google Scholar]

Garavan H, Pendergrass JC, Ross TJ, Stein EA, Risinger RC (2001) Amygdala response to both positively and negatively valenced stimuli. Neuroreport 12: 2779–2783. [PubMed] [Google Scholar]

Gottfried JA, O'Doherty J, Dolan RJ (2002) Appetitive and aversive olfactory learning in humans studied using event-related functional magnetic resonance imaging. J

Neurosci 22: 10829–10837. [PMC free article] [PubMed] [Google Scholar]

Tracey I, Becerra L, Chang I, Breiter H, Jenkins L, et al. (2000) Noxious hot and cold stimulation produce common patterns of brain activation in humans: a functional magnetic resonance imaging study. Neurosci Lett 288: 159–162. [PubMed] [Google Scholar]

Critchley HD, Wiens S, Rotshtein P, Ohman A, Dolan RJ (2004) Neural systems supporting interoceptive awareness. Nat Neurosci 7: 189–195. [PubMed] [Google Scholar]

Phan KL, Wager T, Taylor SF, Liberzon I (2002) Functional neuroanatomy of emotion: a meta-analysis of emotion activation studies in PET and fMRI. Neuroimage 16: 331–348. [PubMed] [Google Scholar]

Huettel SA, Misiurek J, Jurkowski AJ, McCarthy G (2004) Dynamic and strategic aspects of executive processing. Brain Res 1000: 78–84. [PubMed] [Google Scholar]

Eisenberger NI, Lieberman MD, Williams KD (2003) Does rejection hurt? An FMRI study of social exclusion. Science 302: 290–292. [PubMed] [Google Scholar]

Craig AD (2002) How do you feel? Interception: the sense of the physiological condition of the body. Nat Rev Neurosci 3: 655–666. [PubMed] [Google Scholar]

Saxe R, Kanwisher N (2003) People thinking about thinking people. The role of the temporo-parietal junction in "theory of mind". Neuroimage 19: 1835–1842. [PubMed] [Google Scholar]

Van Overwalle F (2009) Social cognition and the brain: a meta-analysis. Hum Brain Mapp 30: 829–858. [PMC free article] [PubMed] [Google Scholar]

Poole KT (2005) Spatial models of parliamentary voting. Cambridge; New

York: Cambridge University Press. xviii, 230 p.

Alford JR, Funk CL, Hibbing JR (2005) Are Political Orientations Genetically Transmitted? American Political Science Review 99: 153–167. [Google Scholar]

Achen C (2002) Parental socialization and rational party identification. Political Behavior 24: 151–170. [Google Scholar]

Draganski B, Gaser C, Busch V, Schuierer G, Bogdahn U, et al. (2004) Neuroplasticity: changes in grey matter induced by training. Nature 427: 311–312. [PubMed] [Google Scholar]

Scholz J, Klein MC, Behrens TE, Johansen-Berg H (2009) Training induces changes in white-matter architecture. Nat Neurosci. [PMC free article] [PubMed]

Woollett K, Maguire EA (2011) Acquiring "the Knowledge" of London's Layout Drives

Structural Brain Changes. Current biology. [PMC free article] [PubMed]

Settle JE, Dawes CT, Fowler JH (2009) The Heritability of Partisan Attachment. Political Research Quarterly 62: 601–613. [Google Scholar]

Fowler JH, Schreiber D (2008) Biology, politics, and the emerging science of human nature. Science 322: 912–914. [PubMed] [Google Scholar]

Cox RW (1996) AFNI: software for analysis and visualization of functional magnetic resonance neuroimages. Comput Biomed Res 29: 162–173. [PubMed] [Google Scholar]

Boynton GM, Engel SA, Glover GH, Heeger DJ (1996) Linear systems analysis of functional magnetic resonance imaging in human V1. J Neurosci 16: 4207–4221. [PMC free article] [PubMed] [Google Scholar]

Lancaster JL, Woldorff MG, Parsons LM, Liotti M, Freitas CS, et al. (2000) Automated Talairach atlas labels for functional brain mapping. Hum Brain Mapp 10: 120–131. [PMC free article] [PubMed] [Google Scholar]

Tuschman, A. (2013). Our political nature: The evolutionary origins of what divides us. Amherst, NY: Prometheus.

Inglehart, R., and Welzel, C. (2005). Modernization, cultural change, and democracy. Cambridge, UK: Cambridge University Press.

Zuckerman, P. (2008). Society without God: What the least religious nations can tell us about contentment. New York: New York University Press.